READER INSTRUCTION
IN
COLLEGES AND UNIVERSITIES

teaching the use of the library

READER INSTRUCTION
IN
COLLEGES AND UNIVERSITIES

teaching the use of the library

HAZEL MEWS

LINNET BOOKS & CLIVE BINGLEY

FIRST PUBLISHED 1972 BY CLIVE BINGLEY LTD
THIS EDITION SIMULTANEOUSLY PUBLISHED IN THE USA
BY LINNET BOOKS, AN IMPRINT OF SHOE STRING PRESS INC,
995 SHERMAN AVENUE, HAMDEN, CONNECTICUT 06514
PRINTED IN GREAT BRITAIN
0-208-01174-9

Contents

ACKNOWLEDGMENTS

I am very grateful to those of my colleagues at the University of Reading who so kindly allowed me to make use both of their ideas and their comments in the chapters of case histories, and to the University Librarian for his encouragement.   HM

1
Introduction

DEFINITION: What is 'reader instruction'? Another currently used term is 'library instruction', which puts the emphasis on the library rather than the reader, and which also suggests to some that library instruction concerns the training of librarians. For the purpose of this introductory handbook 'reader instruction' is taken to mean instruction given to readers to help them make the best use of a library, particularly an academic library of some size and complexity.

The obvious way to learn to use a library might seem to be just to use it, but this is not quite as simple as it appears, and certainly the processes of learning can be speeded up by expert guidance. A large library is frequently described as a storehouse of knowledge; its resources of books, pamphlets, periodicals, reference books, bibliographies, abstracts, newspapers and 'metabooks' (to use a recent designation for the newer non-book materials such as records, tapes, films, microfilms, etc) are painstakingly assembled, classified, catalogued and arranged on the shelves for the benefit of the student. Yet many students find large libraries daunting, and tend to wander round the stacks in a haphazard way and to get the notion that there is 'nothing in the library' of use to them. For the stern realities of writing essays, participating in tutorial discussions and passing examinations they need a systematic approach to finding their materials; a vague trust in serendipity is not enough. This ordered approach to a large library, although not instinctive, is quite easily acquired, and the best way to help readers to acquire it has been occupying the attention of many people in the educational world in recent years. This small book gives information about several of the ways that have been tried, and may serve also as a summary of present trends as seen by one person with several years' experience in the field.

Some librarians regret the emphasis which reader instruction places upon what they regard as a utilitarian approach to libraries; they would prefer to stress the value of the trigger mechanism brought into play when mind meets mind through an encounter in ' the higher browsing '. Others feel that the library's most important role in an over-specialized syllabus lies in bridging the gaps between subjects, and encouraging a life-long habit of using books—and metabooks—for the enrichment of the mental life of the individual. There is no reason why all these aims should not be advanced and encouraged by reader instruction, although not necessarily for all students in all colleges and universities at all times; to accomplish that would be a very considerable undertaking indeed.

BACKGROUND

Reader instruction is not entirely new. Consultation with the scholar librarian of a learned library has taken place since libraries began, and instruction has been provided unobtrusively by enquiry assistants, and in the form of readers' advisory services in public libraries in America and Britain for some time. The introductory talk by the university librarian to new students arriving at the university has long been accepted general practice in the English-speaking academic world, not excluding the countries of the Commonwealth. But the ' information explosion ' which continues to explode, and the great increase in student numbers since the end of the second world war have combined to render the need for instruction more pressing. No longer can the skill to make effective use of the complex resources of a modern academic library be automatically assumed to follow by the exercise of some commonsense working on the rudiments provided by a long familiarity with books at home and at school. Many young people now attending institutions of higher education scarcely use the library at all, other than as a place to sit and write or to meet their friends. This neglect of so great an asset as a large library is seen not only as waste of the great resources that go into creating it, but in a civilization that is largely bookbuilt, such indifference must cause much heart-searching amongst those responsible for national education policies and structures.

The problem was confronted in a practical way by science and industry on some occasions when certain very expensive research turned out to be only a repetition of work already done elsewhere and already recorded in the literature of science. The urgent need to search the literature before embarking upon new work was made manifest. As science is international, this was no merely national problem. The Royal Society of London put the influence of its great prestige behind endeavours to work out a solution to the growing problems of the organization and use of scientific information, when it called the Royal Society Scientific Information Conference in London in June 1948, to be followed ten years later by an International Conference on Scientific Information in Washington. The suggestions of the Royal Society's original working party on training in the use of information have had considerable influence on the pattern of reader instruction outside the field of science as well as within it. After more than twenty years it is enlightening to re-read the conference's original recommendations:

' 11.2 *Training in the use of information*—As part of their education scientists should be instructed in the use of libraries and information services. This should be done at two different stages:

' 11.21 *Undergraduate stage*: A general introduction to the university library and its use should be given by the university staff to first year students. This could take the form of lectures and demonstrations supplemented by suitable publications and films.

' 11.22 *Postgraduate stage*: Postgraduate students should receive detailed instruction in methods of searching and in the formulation of clear requests for scientific information at an early stage in postgraduate work. Instruction in classification schemes, subject indexing and in the use of catalogues, abstracts, bibliographies and reference books should be included. Scien-

9

tists should be trained in giving full, relevant and precise details when specific information is asked for.

'The instruction should be given by the library staff and information officers of the establishment in which the scientist is working, whether it be a university (in which case librarians of local special libraries would also take part) research institution or large industrial firm. Such instruction should form a regular part in introducing every newcomer to a research establishment.

'11.3 *Text-books for bibliographical training*—The conference has concluded that guides and handbooks to scientific literature in the various fields of science would be particularly useful as textbooks for training scientists in the use of bibliographical tools.

'Every effort should be made to encourage publications and films explaining the nature and organization of special libraries and the ways in which they can be most efficiently used by the scientist.' (Report, p 203.)

In Britain a powerful lead in the implementation of these recommendations has been given by the National Lending Library for Science and Technology at Boston Spa. Since 1962 it has conducted many courses in scientific information; originally intended for research students in science, these classes have been made available to university teaching staff and to librarians. They include a number of guided searches for specific information and one very useful topic has been the structure of the literature of science; recently the literature of the social sciences has been included in some of the classes. These courses are of necessity confined to the use of scientific literature, literature that is the same whether it stands on the shelves in Bristol or Boston Spa, Berlin or Bombay. Skills such as the use of a library catalogue or the understanding of classification schemes are not included in the syllabuses of the NLL, but the staff are always at hand for consultation.

What is sauce for the scientific goose is sauce for the humanities gander, and although the problem of the neglect of the literature is not obvious in such practical and concrete ways as in scientific research, there is cause for concern in the disciplines of the arts and social sciences. Repeated regurgitation by students of lecture notes or of a few paragraphs from standard textbooks and a narrow selection of well-known popular surveys, has given concern to those wishing to maintain high academic standards. The Hale report (*Report of the Committee on University Teaching Methods*), published in London in 1964, laid emphasis on the importance of teaching by means of small discussion groups and tutorials in addition to the traditional lecture. It pointed out the consequent result, namely that the student would have to prepare himself to take a really active and individual part in the work of such groups and would therefore find it essential to be able to find relevant material in the university library. In 1967 the Parry report on university libraries in Britain devoted a whole chapter to ' Guidance in the use of libraries ', and made the following specific recommendations:

' We recommend that all students should be given preliminary guidance on the lay-out of the library, its regulations and procedures. At a later stage (the exact timing to be given careful consideration in individual institutions) seminars should be held and lectures given on the use of bibliographical tools, guidance on the literature of the student's own subject, etc.' (Par 504.)

This recommendation in its turn has been much in the minds of British university librarians during the tumultuous years since the publication of the Parry report. Student unrest and protest, general uncertainty as to the future with its growing pressure of student numbers, the physical vulnerability of libraries to vandalism, have all been worries impossible to brush aside. The ever-rising prices of books and journals have to be met at a time when losses and mutilation of the library's volumes are increasing. The old sanctions that were once efficacious in securing the return and replacement of books no longer work, and the individual's attitude to public property has grossly deteriorated. It is not surprising that while librarians have been struggling to maintain the quality of their service against this background, no large and firmly organized schemes of reader instruction have yet emerged. This waiting period has, however, had the advantage of providing time for experimentation with different methods in the various kinds of colleges and universities now emerging from the changing forms of higher education. Experience gained in this period should provide the basis for a more satisfactory pattern of instruction when the times are less turbulent.

The cross-fertilization of ideas between English and American libraries is continuous, and the American idea of the library-college, in which priorities are reversed and, instead of a library in a college there is a college, as it were, built around a library, appeals powerfully to a number of British librarians, who find that tributes paid on public occasions to the important place the library occupies in the institution are not invariably matched by day-to-day support for its needs. The new library-colleges are planned to be built around 'resource centres', rather than libraries in the more conventional sense, and are to contain all kinds of apparatus falling under the category of 'educational technology', and all the resources of computerized information retrieval. These developments match trends that have become evident in many British academic libraries in recent years.

2
Initial problems

Since reader instruction is not yet fully integrated into contemporary higher education systems, the librarian who contemplates providing such instruction is confronted with certain choices to be made, and important decisions to be taken, before he can proceed with any definite plans. He will need to clarify his own mind as to what is not only possible now, but possible to continue in the future, as to what is best not only for his library and the college or university community it serves but also for the role that college or university will have to play in the wider regional and national plans of education now emerging. He will also need to talk the matter over with other members of the college community, lecturing and library staff and students as well as with his own committee.

There is a growing pool of experience in library instruction into which he can dip his bucket. Some of the publications recording this experience are listed in the bibliography at the end of this book. The majority of recent papers give information about courses in individual libraries, usually confined to one subject or a group of similar subjects; a good deal of information concerning experiments with different audio-visual aids has also appeared in professional journals during the last few years. It will be found from reading a selection of these papers that reader instruction means different things to different people, and that it is given by a variety of methods, both traditional and audio-visual, and at various levels of thoroughness. Most of the accounts are factual and include statistics of attendance at the classes, but for the greater part they maintain a scientific detachment from any consideration of the actual human and social situations in which the classes are given. Since many teachers of library skills find themselves in unfamiliar situations, they welcome frank, first-hand accounts of actual classroom experiences as being particularly helpful to them; for instance, the sympathetic psychological adjustments made in the highly specialized library-integrated seminars for teachers of maladjusted children at the University of London Institute of Education (Bristow) have many lessons to offer instructors in other subjects. As time goes on this lack may be remedied, but in the meantime the librarian planning library instruction may well feel unprepared concerning the human problems, and may seek reassurance from his colleagues.

An indication of the kind of initial decisions mentioned above as confronting the librarian planning to begin reader instruction courses may perhaps be given by setting some of them out in the form of questions he might have to ask himself; in the following list these are arranged under headings indicating the groups of people concerned as well as the different practical aspects of the organization involved:

ACADEMIC/TEACHING STAFF

Are the teaching staff interested in library instruction, and do they believe it to have value?

Do they wish their own students to have instruction, and will they co-operate in any future plans, *eg* by suggestions as to content and timing and by encouraging their students to come along?

Would they prefer: a) To give the instruction themselves? b) To co-operate with the library staff in giving it? c) To have the library staff alone give it?

Can answers to these questions be best obtained by approaching faculty boards, departmental heads or individuals, and should the approach be formal (in writing) or informal?

STUDENTS

Do the students *need* instruction?

At what levels do they need it?

Do the students realise their need and *want* library instruction, or are they inclined to think it is: a) a burden of busywork devised by fussy librarians? b) a subtle form of indoctrination or additional load devised by the establishment?

Can and should their reluctance be overcome? How?

Should instruction be provided for all students or for some only? What should be the governing factors?

If only a few students benefit from instruction has this sufficient ultimate value to justify the use of the resources needed?

LIBRARY STAFF

Is the library staff as a whole enthusiastic, lukewarm or antagonistic to the new work?

Are there enough competent assistants to tackle the work?

Who should do the teaching? In a subject-specialized library should it all be done by the subject specialists, or should others be brought in?

How can time be arranged in the library's work time-table both for classes and for preparation?

Can the present staff carry this task indefinitely or should provision for new staff be made?

CONTENT OF THE COURSES

What exactly do the students need to be taught that concerns a) the individual library, b) the subjects being studied and that c) will encourage them to continue to use libraries after they have left college?

METHODS USED IN THE COURSES

Should lectures, seminars and/or tutorials be used?

Should audio-visual methods be used and what special purpose should they serve?

Should there be a combination of both personal teaching and audio-visual aids each supplementing the other?

If audio-visual aids are used, is there a 'media department' with the necessary equipment and technical expertise on the spot or near by?

Should films, tape/slides, etc, be made, bought or borrowed, or a combination of all three?

PLACE

Where shall the courses be held, a) In the library itself? b) In a library lecture or seminar room? c) In a central university lecture-hall? d) In a departmental room? e) In the media centre?

What number of students will need to be seated for each section of the courses?

Will there be technical apparatus and staff available for showing films, etc, on the days required?

TIME

When shall the courses he held? a) At what times in the students' university years? b) At what times in the students' timetables? c) How can times be chosen so that they fit in with departmental timetables and commitments? Will the departments and/or the faculty offices help in this?

BOOKS

If books are needed in the classes, can they be borrowed from the library's present bookstock without inconveniencing other readers?

If books need to be conveyed to departments or central lecture rooms and returned afterwards, can this be easily arranged?

Should special copies of certain books be purchased for use in the courses? What funds could be used? Where could these books be kept between courses?

To pose such questions is not, of course, to answer them; only the librarian of an individual library can make the necessary decisions and try to foresee the consequences. An American writer on education has recently suggested that at the heart of the problem of modern education lies a failure to think seriously about purposes or consequences, ' the failure of people at every level to ask why they are doing what they are doing or to inquire into the consequences '. One thing is certain in the field of reader instruction—if the librarian does not voluntarily confront these problems in the beginning, experience will soon demand decisions from him.

16

3
Organization of the courses

STRUCTURE: However excellent the subject content of the instruction given, it will need to be supported by some kind of structure, although this need not necessarily be too firmly erected and permanent. Institutions vary greatly in their practice of including reader instruction in the educational programme itself: some colleges go so far as to examine students in library skills, some definitely require attendance at library instruction courses and print this requirement in their calendars, some offer courses but permit students to take them or leave them, and some wait for the staff or students themselves to initiate requests for instruction. Not only do institutions vary but departments within the same institution often take widely different views on this question, and again these views may change with change of personnel, so that overall arrangements that are too rigid tend to break down in practice.

To provide some kind of framework for discussing organization it is convenient to consider the structure as having three levels, partly due to the Royal Society Conference tradition, and partly because it is convenient and one can argue that all sub-levels can be ultimately connected with the basic three.

The lowest or foundation level provides a general introduction to the individual library, the next level brings in more subject and bibliographical material and the third caters for the needs of advanced and research students. A turret or side-wings added to the basic structure may be thought of as giving room for special types of instruction, experiments in new ways of arousing interest, or even gimmicks, if gimmicks can serve a useful purpose.

It has long been standard practice in many universities for the librarian himself (or, occasionally, herself) to give an introductory talk about the services of the library. This usually takes place during an 'orientation' or 'freshers' conference' week, before the commencement of the first term of a new session. The librarian often appears on the platform with the Deans of the Faculties and other university dignitaries. The value of the occasion obviously varies with the institution and the librarian's platform personality, but, although the students may not remember very much from his talk, they will at least have seen the librarian himself and, it is to be hoped, they will gather the impression both that the library is an important part of the academic institution, and that the library staff will be willing and anxious to help the students.

Such introductory talks are often followed by tours of the library building. If merely left to chance after a vague invitation from the librarian to 'come along', these tours can become wild scrambles of small parties on the run round a large institution, anxious only to head off the party in front and to avoid involuntary fusion with the party behind. An obvious way to avoid this is to space the tours out during the orientation week or the first few days of term, putting up notices about them in all possible places and letting the students' union know well in advance so that the tours can be listed in the programmes circulated to all freshers. Then, for example, six tours a day can be offered to those who assemble at a given point and a set time (*eg* on the hour), and members of the library staff can be at the ready to act as guides, with some kind of briefing given beforehand to new members of the library staff.

It is easy to expect too much of such tours, but they do perform one service of inalienable value—they give the student the actual physical and psychological experience of being in the library building—for him it can never again be the first time of entry into what may be regarded as a large and forbidding edifice. He can also at least be shown where to enrol as a reader and where to make his enquiries, and he can be handed a copy of the library's *Handbook* or *Guide,* which it is still standard practice for academic libraries to print, or near-print each session.

AUDIO-VISUAL AIDS TO INSTRUCTION

Recently some libraries have preferred to replace these tours with a film of the library intended to serve the same introductory purpose, while other libraries use films to supplement instead of to replace the tours. Such films can be shown on a continuous performance basis or at stated times of the day, all depending upon the rooms, the apparatus and the staff available.

The whole subject of audio-visual or mechanical aids to library instruction, either to be used at this initial level or later, is in that state of innovatory chaos out of which some order will presumably emerge in time. Many universities and colleges, especially those with media centres, are engaged on making and re-making films, tape/slides, videotapes and so forth, and many articles appear on their activities. Research is also in progress into other types of equipment for guiding readers, witness the experiments with electronic library guides at Hatfield Polytechnic, financed by the Leverhulme Trust, and the Massachusetts Institute of Technology's Project Intrex, an experimental model engineering library with many kinds of new apparatus. It is obviously desirable, and is indeed intended, that other libraries should benefit from these experiments.

Audio-visual aids can also be produced on a co-operative basis, and used in many different institutions, supplemented where need be by local material. A group of British librarians recently embarked upon a co-operative scheme for the production of tape/slide guides to library services, and began by appointing working parties to produce the following:

Guide to general literature searching techniques
Guide to abstracting and indexing services
Guide to report literature
Guide to British official publications
Guide to patent literature
Guide to the literature of chemistry
Guide to the literature of electrical engineering

Guide to the literature of medicine
Guide to the literature of mechanical engineering
Guide to the literature of the social services
Guide to the use of Beilstein
Guide to the use of *Chemical abstracts.*

This group recently agreed to work in association with the New Media Sub-Committee of the Standing Conference on National and University Libraries (SCONUL). Aslib also has an active Audio-Visual Group, which is preparing a directory of libraries and producers of audio-visual aids which have material available to outside users; the group is also producing a *Newsletter.* The Library Association has issued a catalogue of films and filmstrips on librarianship and related subjects, and the National Council for Educational Technology's Higher Education Programmes' Information Service is collecting ' details of unpublished learning materials produced in institutions of higher education which would be suitable for use outside the originating institution ', and it recently issued an experimental *Catalogue of materials available for exchange.* Furthermore, there is in London a National Committee for Audio-Visual Aids in Education with a National Audio-Visual Aids Centre offering courses in producing these aids. In the USA, the Council for Library Resources supports many American developments. Commercially produced films and slides introducing students to libraries and to reference books are available for hire, possibly more readily in the new world than the old.

The difficulty for librarians who would like to borrow, hire, buy, exchange or even view such aids is that catalogues, or even the opinions of other colleagues, are not an adequate basis for choice; it is obviously desirable that there should be central national depositories where specimens of all such aids could be housed and made readily accessible for viewing. This is at the moment under discussion in Britain.

The present state of the art renders it impossible to say with certainty what the best use of these teaching aids will be, but throughout this book it will be tacitly assumed that their assistance can and will be called upon where appropriate in the various stages of library instruction.

THE SECOND STAGE

After the student feels some familiarity with the library—the layout of the building, the hours of opening, the rules and regulations—he may begin to borrow books. Most of his early reading will consist of publications recommended by his lecturers and appearing on the lists handed to him by his department. If these lists are bibliographically accurate and if he is used to a good school or public library, he should be able to get what he needs without much difficulty; anyway most of his material is likely to be in the special undergraduate collections now to be found in so many academic libraries. There is certainly nothing intrinsically difficult about using a library at this level—little more than the equivalent of finding out the way to buy a railway ticket to a known destination, for which one need understand little about the railway system or the topography of the country.

Some librarians believe that at this stage actual instruction should be given in the elements of a catalogue card, ' see also ' references, alphabetization, the filling in of reserve forms, headings for government publications, etc etc, but the difficulty is that not only is such information intrinsically dull and boring, but the student considers it irrelevant until he actually needs to use it, until, for instance, he needs to find a book by an author named M'Whirter and finds himself standing before the drawers of catalogue cards under M. There would seem therefore to be a definite case for providing such information by means other than verbal instruction.

Printed library handbooks or guides are often chosen as the places for practical information about the catalogue (*eg* treatment of the German umlaut, headings chosen for periodicals and conferences, cards included for holdings of branch libraries, etc), and strategically placed notices on the catalogue cabinets or nearby ensure the conjunction of time and place of relevance. Such notices and displayed explanations can be very useful if well-designed and kept up-to-date and clean, but their use is sometimes thought to spoil the line of the catalogue cabinets. The Cambridge University Library's Management Research Unit plans to undertaken studies ' of the effect of such methods as information leaflets, sign posting within libraries, clear labelling of subject collections, etc upon the effectiveness of reader use of libraries '. Sophisticated electronic or other point-of-need devices might be of help. If instruction at greater length is thought desirable, use might be made of programmed teaching machines. Printed programmed texts, like those by Felicia Webster and T W Burrell, are now available in English, and sections of these could, where appropriate, be translated into foreign languages for overseas students. By making such machines available at the point-of-use, libraries would also cater for the shy student who does not like to ask for help, or for the forgetful student who has asked several times already and does not wish to confess that he has forgotten.

In all this instruction in what is basically cataloguing practice, the information imparted is strictly practical and the intention is to smooth the way for the reader to find what he desires to find; this is obvious to librarians themselves and also, to a lesser extent, to mature readers, but the young student often finds it all very irritating because he cannot see the wood for the trees. More in accord with the concept of books as treasures of the mind, collected in a particular storehouse called the library of the University of X, is a second level of reader instruction that gives a brief introduction to the *understanding* of the way the particular storehouse of such treasures is organized, with, possibly, some actual practice in locating there specific publications connected with the subjects being studied. Most second-year students and some late first-year students should be ready for such help, but it is difficult to arrange it for all of these in a large college at the right psychological moment, even if that moment could always be reliably calculated. The attempt can be made for all students, however, by means of brief stencilled guides made freely available, or by audio-visual aids providing instruction at this level.

Additional live instruction can be given and it may take the form of, say, two seminars for students interested in the same group of subjects. The first seminar can consist of a general introduction to the way the library has tackled its problems of arranging and recording tens of hundreds or thousands of books; brief library projects or exercises can be handed out at this class-meeting, to be completed before the next meeting. The second of the two meetings is the occasion for a discussion on how the students handled their individual projects. If a different project is handed to each student, the discussion at the second seminar enables each student to share the experiences of the others. Although such library exercises can quite easily be drawn up by librarians working from the books themselves, with no expert knowledge of the subject in hand, it is really quite difficult to produce questions that do not seem to some students to be rather contrived and remote from what they are able to envisage as the object of the exercise. More will be said about this problem in the discussion on the subject content of courses of library instruction (page 30*ff*).

Another way of introducing library instruction is for it to be the subject of one talk in a series covering a much wider topic, such as ' communication ', ' the information explosion ' or ' writing essays and dissertations ', the kind of short series often devised by academic departments or faculties. Sequences of talks on these lines are often co-operative efforts involving more than one department and both teaching and library staff; they can, if well prepared and co-ordinated, be of value to all concerned, students and staff alike.

THE THIRD STAGE

The third stage must cover the subject literature in some depth and give guidance that should prove useful for collecting material needed both in a final-year paper and in a full-scale research project. The course can be of any length, from a short sequence of two or three intensive classes to a regular period once a week during a whole term, enabling more time to be devoted to the various categories of the literature. In certain cases the classes can be very closely integrated with the subject course itself, but this must depend upon local circumstances, and it is best if such close integration grows naturally from smaller beginnings that are actually seen to be valuable and worth expanding. The teaching staff may wish to conduct the classes themselves, but will sometimes welcome help and support from the library staff. Librarians need to be able and willing to adjust their pre-conceived ideas and plans to meet the precise needs of the different departments as they gradually unfold.

There is a special difficulty with regard to overseas students who arrive in the country to do advanced work but who, having received no instruction at the earlier stages, find the third stage too difficult to encompass. Here mechanical aids can play a special part in repeating for them the earlier instruction they may have missed. The possibility of re-playing and re-hearing recorded instruction also helps them at a period when their command of the language makes it unlikely that they can absorb information at the same pace as those whose mother tongue is used as the medium. Some thought might be given to the question of translating the ' introductions to the library ', or devising adaptations of them—a variation of Apna Hi Ghar Samajhiye for the university library—but this would probably require considerable pooling of resources between a group of interested institutions.

SPECIAL ACTIVITIES

Outside the main three-level structure a place can be made for special activities designed to spread knowledge and love of books and better understanding of libraries. Literary quizzes, information panels, essay competitions with book tokens as prizes, teach-ins, discussions connected with specially notable book exhibitions—all have been tried in different libraries and talked about in others. They demand much staff time and ingenuity and the first fine careless rapture is not easily repeated, but they do offer variety and they give scope for inventive members of the library staff or of the other sections of the academic community to try out a new idea. They can also give opportunities for co-operation between the academic, public and special libraries in the area, whose staff meet only at the level of mutual borrowing or at the branch of the professional association, whereas their work could be fruitfully extended through a common interest in reader instruction wisely interpreted.

THE TIME

Much stress is laid on the necessity for reader instruction courses to be arranged at just the right time of the student's academic career, but no one who has had experience of trying to insert extra periods into a college timetable has any illusions that one can just pick and choose. Vacations, examinations, laboratory work, field work, concerts, playreadings, the 'rag' and, more recently, demonstrations, all have to be taken account of in addition to the already heavy lecture timetables; if even standard courses have to be arranged by a computer how small a chance has library instruction. The obvious expedient of holding classes in the evening or on Saturdays is unpopular with all concerned, and attendances, unless the college runs other courses at such times, are likely to be poor. If the courses are required by regulation, certain periods will be officially allotted to them, but otherwise departments and faculty offices are the only sources of knowledge of the students' timetables sufficiently detailed to be able to make suggestions. Lecturers are also able to make the classes known to their own students and to urge them to attend.

THE PLACE

The place in which reader instruction is given may have to be dictated by the location of any apparatus, such as a projector, that is to be used. Apart from such practicalities, the necessity for being in the library building itself varies with the content of the course; sometimes it is better for psychological reasons to hold meetings in departmental rooms already familiar to the students. Heavy emphasis is at present laid upon informal surroundings and a relaxed atmosphere, and although this fashion may pass it has to be remembered in planning seminars in the 1970's. Some librarians feel a sense of disloyalty to the library if they go outside it, both literally and metaphorically, and more flexibility is obviously desirable in this ivory-tower mentality. Much depends upon the layout of the buildings on the campus and expediency will often have to be the guide.

It is of practical importance that the room should be firmly booked well in advance. The spectacle of two classes simultaneously claiming the same room is amusing in retrospect but it is not an experience to be recommended; it also provokes irritation and sometimes ill-will in some quarters. Readers who usually use a particular room should also be remembered and notices put up in advance warning them that their sanctuary will be invaded at such-and-such a time. Nor can it always be relied upon that the room will contain the requisite number of chairs, blackboard, chalk and rubber in addition to the projector and/or other apparatus; these must all be checked. The library is not usually geared into the university machinery that is accustomed to provide such indispensable articles automatically, and the responsibility lies with the library staff to take the initiative in these arrangements.

BIBLIOGRAPHICAL TOOLS

If students are to be taught to use certain books it is obvious that at least some of these should be available for examination, either in the classroom or in the reference section or on the shelves of the main collection that afternoon, and arrangements must be duly made. If there is too much concentration on a few books this again creates difficulties for other readers. It may sometimes be necessary to buy multiple copies, but since book grants are increasingly strained this is difficult, and it is scarcely likely that a duplicate set of *Chemical abstracts* or *Biological abstracts* could be justified for such a purpose.

Where applicable, one way round this difficulty is to suggest various sources for finding information and to point out that in the library, as elsewhere in human society, the very afternoon when the individual wants some particular article of public property, another individual is using it. The development of resourcefulness in looking for information in more than one place is one of the positive gains that can come from library instruction, but it certainly requires forethought on the part of the instructor and must be prepared for well in advance. Both short term and long term arrangements to provide the necessary bibliographical tools need to be worked out, remembering that new tools and revised editions of old tools are being published all the time.

STAFFING

Who shall give the instruction? It need not necessarily be the library staff, for there would seem to be three possibilities, in addition to getting outside experts to come in, or sending the students to some other institution such as the National Lending Library for Science and Technology:

1) The academic teaching staff
2) The library and/or information staff
3) A combination of both.

As personal views and interests are closely involved, practice will differ in different institutions, but one constant remains— if the academic teaching staff lacks interest in or conviction about the value of the enterprise, it is not likely to prosper very rapidly. The main responsibility for the intellectual content of a student's university or college course is rightly and naturally in the hands of his lecturers, and if they are not convinced of the need for or value of library instruction, the doubts will influence their students; even though the lecturers may not actually discourage participation, the absence of active encouragement at this stage will be interpreted to mean that the matter is of scant importance and the classes can be ignored without a further thought.

If the lecturers themselves give the instruction, so much the better, but librarians must expect and should surely welcome the opportunity to help with making books available, supplying stencilled lists, and so on.

Another advantage of lecturer-participation is that it avoids the pitfall for an unwary librarian of inadvertently interfering in matters of intellectual controversy. It is generally agreed that, professionally speaking, a librarian should have no politics or religion, and it follows that, vis-à-vis his teaching colleagues, he should not take up a position in any current highly-charged learned debate which would radically oppose that held by those teaching in the relevant department or, worse still, by just some of those teaching in that department. It is not necessary to enlarge on the difficulties that might follow.

If members of the library staff do the teaching, either alone or in co-operation with the teaching staff, they must be chosen carefully. If ' reader instructors ' or ' orientation librarians ' specially recruited for the task are not available, the subject specialists or information officers are the obvious people to provide instruction in their own specialities. In these cases it can very often be dovetailed in with actual information work, so as to be less obtrusive and less formally organized than if the tuition is given, say, by someone from the acquisitions department. A subject-specialized library is therefore an easier place in which to arrange reader instruction than a highly centralized general library.

To many librarians, the teaching situation is an unfamiliar one, and one from which they have deliberately chosen to remain apart by becoming librarians rather than teachers. Briefing sessions are helpful for those who have no experience and who do not know what they can expect in what is unknown territory for many. These sessions can be given by those with most knowledge of the situations to be faced and of what is needed by the students.

Because of these difficulties it may be hard to find enough people willing to undertake the task for more than a couple of classes, and the teaching may have to be continued by just a few. Obviously, however, one person will need to plan the courses so that there is no overlapping, and at least one person must know what is going on in the project as a whole. There will also be a need for continual interest, encouragement and support from the highest levels: this is no ordinary routine task that is required of those who undertake it, and they have the additional discomfiture of finding themselves rather outside the accepted circles of traditional librarianship.

4

Subject content of the courses

The librarian needs to think long and carefully about the subject content of the courses he proposes to initiate, for whatever the form in which they are presented, their content is of the greatest importance.

What exactly do students need to know in order to use books, libraries and information services to better effect? The answer can be explored under the following four main headings:

1) The use of the individual library

2) The structure of the literature of the student's subject

3) The background of the national library network and specialized information sources

4) Other aids (writing dissertations; publication; asking for information, etc).

Throughout his involvement with reader instruction, the librarian needs to keep a check on any latent tendency to spend time on purely professional preoccupations; consistency in the use of commas or full-stops on the catalogue card may interest him but will bore the reader; he must ever be on guard against any subconscious inclination to regard student-readers as embryo librarians. He will also need to divest himself of his long familiarity with the inner clockwork of libraries and try to see them as others see them. His habit of using bibliographical terms precisely is not shared by the reader, and since many of such terms are ordinary everyday words—title-page, periodical, serial, imprint, location, pamphlet—and not the more esoteric vocabulary of science, the two sides of the dialogue do not even realize that they are talking different languages; it takes a little time for adjustment to be achieved and real communication to begin. Lastly, the librarian needs repeatedly to remind himself that the courses should not only have relevance to the students' needs but, as far as possible, they should be seen to have relevance, and the end should not be lost sight of in over-concentration on the means.

Some indication of various ways of conveying information about what it is convenient to call the ' mechanical ' side of the use of the library has already been given above (p 21), but here it may be helpful to consider what basic information should be covered by the tape/slides, notices on the cabinets, leaflets, and, to take the most widely used medium, the printed library guide. The following factual information should at least be given:

A plan of the library buildings; any very large building will need many supplementary ' you are here ' plans.

List and location of special rooms and special collections.

Hours of opening.

Rules and regulations, including those governing borrowing of books.

Classification scheme used.

Whereabouts of special sequences for oversize books.

List and locations of catalogues (*eg*, author, dictionary, classified; periodicals, theses).

Specimen lay-out of catalogue card with explanation; particularly clear indication of call marks.

Arrangement in the catalogue drawers (alphabetization, Macs, umlauts, etc).

Headings used for special categories of publications—government publications; conferences, etc.

Periodicals—arrangement in catalogues and on shelves, unbound periodicals.

Pamphlets and newspapers.

Microfilms and microfilm readers, microfiches, etc.

List and location of special services (*eg* inter-library loans, reserved books, photographic copies).

Where to go for different kinds of information (general enquiries, information officers, etc).

List of library staff.

List of the library's own publications.

Such facts remain facts with no co-ordinated meaning, and the recommendation about library instruction expressed at the high level of parliamentary committees must surely have been concerned with imparting a deeper understanding of the way a large library is organized and co-ordinated, so that the student can make an intelligent instead of a blind use of it. Classification is a case in point: many students and academic staff are inclined to waste time and intellectual energy in doing battle with their library's classification scheme, which does not take into sufficient account their own department's subject links.

Few librarians have many illusions about the perfection of the scheme they have inherited or even chosen themselves, nor can they have complete faith in the uniformity of the decisions taken by successive classifiers over the years; but most librarians are willing to consider the opinions of subject specialists and to make such adjustments as do not upset the integrity of the scheme or the needs of other users. However, the experience of being manoeuvred into defending Dewey as against another scheme used in X-College which is, by hearsay, much more satisfactory, or of declining the offer of a brand new scheme to be drawn up by Dr Y provided the librarian undertakes to reclassify the whole library, is not very productive. Often the trouble lies in a misunderstanding of what the classification scheme is attempting to do, a task concerned with the ramifications of all human knowledge rather than the interests, long term or temporary, of a university department in a certain country at a certain time. An explanation along these lines can lead to a change in outlook, and this angle enables some students to see that the whole thing makes some sense, even if, in their opinion, not very good sense. An example of such an approach is provided by the following extract from a stencilled guide handed out to students in the Faculty of Science in one British university using Dewey; it has proved fairly efficacious in actual practice, but it is repeated here less as a model than as a starting point for improvement and adaptation to individual circumstances:

'Books in a library can be arranged on the shelves in many ways—for example, by colour of binding, by size, by date of receipt, by the author's name, and so on, but it is obviously convenient to have most of the books in a university library arranged according to the subject about which they are written. As books are the records of human knowledge, this virtually means an arrangement, or 'classification' of human knowledge. There are many schemes for the subject classification of books (Bliss, Library of Congress, etc) and all of them have both advantages and disadvantages. The one chosen at ———— is the Dewey Decimal Classification and many students will find that this is the same scheme as was used in their own school library and their local public library. Dewey divides knowledge into the following ten main classes:

- 000 General works
- 100 Philosophy
- 200 Religion
- 300 Social sciences
- 400 Language
- 500 Pure science
- 600 Technology
- 700 The Arts
- 800 Literature
- 900 History

The scheme then sub-divides these main classes into more and more detailed schedules; to illustrate the way this works we may take the main classes 500 (Pure science) and 600 (Technology) to their second figure divisions:

500 *Pure Science*	600 *Technology*
510 Mathematics	610 Medical sciences
520 Astronomy	620 Engineering
530 Physics	630 Agriculture
540 Chemistry and allied sciences	640 Home economics
550 Earth sciences	650 Business
560 Palaeontology	660 Chemical technology
570 Anthropology and biology	670 Manufactures

2

580 Botanical sciences	680 Other manufactures
590 Zoological sciences	690 Building construction

As examples of the next step in sub-division we set out the 530 (Physics) and 540 (Chemistry) tables taken to the third figure sections:

530 *Physics*	540 *Chemistry*
531 Mechanics of solids	541 Physical and theoretical
532 Mechanics of fluids	542 Chemical laboratories
533 Mechanics of gases	543 Analytical chemistry
534 Sound	544 Qualitative analysis
535 Optics	545 Quantitative analysis
536 Heat	546 Inorganic chemistry
537 Electricity and electronics	547 Organic chemistry
538 Magnetism	548 Crystallography
539 Modern physics	549 Mineralogy

The sub-divisions continue further and further, with a decimal point after the first three figures, to break up a long number. This Dewey number is the one stamped at the bottom of the spine of the book so that it can be read as the book stands on the shelf. As it is a number referring to the *subject* with which a book deals, there may be several books with exactly the same number; for example, all books which are general works about 'Sound' will be stamped with the number 534. Books with the same classification number are arranged on the shelf alphabetically according to their authors' surnames.

It is not necessary for the student to have any detailed knowledge of the Dewey Decimal Classification scheme, but he may find it useful to memorize the numbers of the subjects in which he is particularly interested, *eg* Electronic computers 510.7834; Leguminosae 583.32.'

For the humanities and social sciences different examples again can be used, for instance, after the table of the ten main classes, the following can be substituted for the science tables:

' The scheme then sub-divides these main classes into more and more detailed schedules; to illustrate the way in which this

34

works we may take the 300 (Social sciences) and 900 (History) classes to their second figure divisions:

300	*Social sciences*	900	*History*
310	Statistics	910	Geography, travels, descrip-
320	Political science		tion
330	Economics	920	Biography
340	Law	930	Ancient history
350	Public administration	940	Europe
360	Social welfare	950	Asia
370	Education	960	Africa
380	Public service & utilities	970	North America
390	Custom & folklore	980	South America
		990	Other parts of the world

As examples of the next step in sub-division we set out the 320 (Political science) and 840 (French literature) tables to the third figure:

320	*Political science*	840	*French literature*
321	Forms of state	841	French poetry
322	State and church	842	French drama
323	State and individuals	843	French fiction
324	Suffrage and elections	844	French essays
325	Migration & colonization	845	French oratory
326	Slavery	846	French letters
327	Foreign relations	847	French satire & humour
328	Legislation	848	French miscellany
329	Political parties	849	Provençal & Catalan

The sub-divisions continue further, if necessary, with a decimal point after the first three figures, to break up a long number. One much-used further sub-division is the arrangement of literature in periods; to take English drama as an example, the period divisions are:

822	*English drama*
822.1	Early English period (1066-1400)
822.2	Pre-Elizabethan period (1400-1558)
822.3	Elizabethan period (1558-1625)
822.4	Post-Elizabethan period (1625-1702)
822.5	Queen Anne period (1702-1745)

822.6   Later 18th century (1745-1800)
822.7   Early 19th century (1800-1837)
822.8   Victorian period (1837-1900)
822.91   20th century

The Dewey number is the one stamped at the bottom of the spine of the book so that it can be read as it stands on the shelf. As it is a number referring to the *subject* with which a book deals, there may be several books with exactly the same number, for example, all books about Virgil will be stamped with the number 873.1. Books with the same number are arranged on the shelves in the alphabetical order of their authors' surnames.

It is not necessary for the student to have any detailed knowledge of the Dewey Decimal Classification scheme, but he may find it useful to memorize the numbers of subjects in which he is particularly interested, *eg* Communism 335.43; Poetry of W B Yeats 821.912; Fascist Italy 945.091; England under the Stuarts 942.06.'

The examples chosen must follow the practice of the individual library and it is useful that they should reflect any special subject interests pursued in the college.

Similar basic explanations can be worked out for UDC, Library of Congress, Bliss, and indeed any other classification scheme or combination of classification schemes used.

Just as it is helpful for both library and reader that it should be known that classification is really a very complicated undertaking, upon which many minds have laboured, and that, by and large, the schemes work if the basis of them is grasped, so it also helps if the reader has some idea of the magnitude of the library's problem in arranging and keeping track of the books. Again the following is put forward as a suggestion; it is intended to help the reader stand back from the problem for a brief second to see it whole and, incidentally, to introduce the need for rules and regulations:

'*Arrangement of the library*
The library contains over 350,000 books, pamphlets, theses manuscripts, etc, and the problem of organizing them is ob-

viously a large one. To add to the complexity of the situation, about 21,000 new books are added each year, and there are also nearly 3,500 periodicals coming in, some weekly, some monthly, some quarterly. Books are also borrowed and taken away for reading in the halls of residence and at home (about 134,000 were borrowed last year), and they are also taken off the shelves and used on the reading-tables on the six floors of the library building during many hours of every day. To keep track of all the individual books and journals is, therefore, no small task. The rules drawn up to ensure that order is maintained in such a large collection used by both students and staff are set out in the *Library handbook* issued each year; every student needs a copy of this—he will also find in it a plan of the library, hours of opening, etc.'

The actual sub-arrangement on the shelves should be made clear by tier and shelf guides. The usual public library practice of stamping the Cutter number or the first three letters of the author's name beneath the classification number on the spine of each volume is not always followed in academic libraries, where the larger collections render it even more necessary; sometimes regard for the appearance of the spine has precluded any library mark on it at all. It is frequently difficult for a trained librarian to decide in a particular case of a corporate publication which body has been chosen as the author for the main entry in the catalogue and therefore as the name for sub-filing on the shelves, so the poor reader is lost indeed when he is confronted with 95 shelves of volumes bearing the number 942.006 with no other indication of their arrangement; some may be in sets of a shelf or two, but many are individual publications. This is not a problem which reader instruction should try to overcome; a more direct change of practice is obviously necessary.

Nearly every reader confuses the terms ' classification ' ' cataloguing ' and ' indexing ', and it helps to make the exact meanings of these words clear at the outset of reader instruction.

Practically every library has more than one catalogue, although a list of them is not always exhibited in the catalogue hall itself, a tour of inspection being required before one can see what is there. Until the reader realizes that there *are* different kinds of catalogues, he will naturally turn to the first at hand, so for his better understanding of the library he needs to get the purposes of the various catalogues differentiated once and for all in the library he uses. Something on the lines of the following may serve as a basis; the features peculiar to one library and to a group of students of agriculture have been left in as a reminder that every library will have to incorporate its own variations:

' Orderly arrangement of the books on the shelves on the library's six floors is not enough, it is also necessary to have in one place some record or ' index ' of the contents of the library, and this takes the form of a catalogue on cards filed in the battery of catalogue cabinets in the main hall. These cards give bibliographical details (*ie* author, title, publisher, edition, date, etc) about the individual publications in the library's possession, such details being recorded in accordance with internationally accepted cataloguing rules. Publications not arranged on the shelves of the main collection are yet included in the catalogues, namely the older books in the ' reserve ' collection, the pamphlets filed in cabinets at the back of the ground floor, the books in special collections (*eg* Overstone and Cole) and the manuscripts and theses kept in special places. The catalogues also include temporary cards for some items awaiting full cataloguing.

The library has several catalogues covering different fields, but those that will most concern the student in the Faculty of Agriculture will be:

1) the author catalogue   2) the subject catalogues
3) the periodicals catalogues   4) the agricultural pamphlets catalogues.

' *The author catalogue*
This is the type of catalogue most familiar to students; in it the details of each book, pamphlet, thesis, etc, are typed on

cards arranged alphabetically, by the surnames of their authors. This is simple enough when the author is an individual, *eg* ' FREAM, William ', but more complicated when the author is a society, institution or government department, *ie* a ' corporate author '. Catalogue cards for publications of institutions, societies, conferences, etc, are filed under the official name of the body concerned; reports issued by official government departments are catalogued under the official name of the country, sub-divided by the name of the department or office, *eg*:

AMERICAN SOCIETY OF ANIMAL SCIENCE

CANADA. *Department of agriculture*

GREAT BRITAIN. *Agricultural research council.*

INTERNATIONAL CONGRESS OF AGRICULTURAL ENGINEERING

The author catalogue is the obvious one to consult if the student knows the name of the author of the book he wants. On the catalogue card filed under the author's name he will find the book's ' call mark ' (Dewey number) which will enable him to locate the book on the shelf. If the publication is not kept on the open shelves the card will indicate this and the reader should consult one of the assistants working at the enquiry desk.

Sometimes, however, the student will need a book dealing with a certain subject but he will not know the names of authors writing on that subject. In this case he should consult the subject catalogues.'

Subject catalogues in their various forms (classified, alphabetic-subject, dictionary and so on) are more difficult for students to consult. The following notes give no more than a faint suggestion of one method of approach. An additional aid can be provided by a supply of stencilled leaflets on ' how to use the subject index ' to be constantly available near the catalogue cabinets; leaflets have the added advantage of being useful as a place for noting down any relevant subject headings or long call marks as the reader finds them in his search.

' *The subject catalogues*

In the subject catalogues the cards are arranged alphabetically under subject headings; a few examples of the kinds of headings used are:

AGRICULTURAL CHEMICALS

AGRICULTURE—Economic aspects

BEANS, Diseases

BOTANY, Economic

DAIRYING

HORTICULTURE—Film catalogues

MICROBIOLOGY—Laboratory manuals

SOIL-SURVEYS

There will often be several cards with the same subject heading, and the sub-arrangement is alphabetical by the names of the authors writing on that same subject. Subject headings covering wide topics are sub-divided, as in the ' MICROBIOLOGY —Laboratory manuals' example given above. The cards also give the call numbers in the same way as the cards in the author catalogue.'

This explanation will not take on real meaning until the student actually uses the catalogue, but it does convey the indispensable minimum he needs to start using it.

With science, technology, agriculture and engineering students it is important that very early in their career they get clear in their minds what a ' periodical ' really is (grasping the essential point that it comes out at intervals and plans to continue publication indefinitely), and that they realize the periodicals catalogue is not an index to the individual papers in all the library's journals, for in this respect hope springs eternal. An example of a lead-in for agriculture students follows:

' The periodicals catalogues

Agriculture students have to use periodicals a good deal and they will need to get to know very soon which periodicals the library takes and how far back the set of each periodical goes. This information can be found in the periodicals catalogues.

The most frequently used section of the periodicals catalogues is the one arranged alphabetically by the title of the periodical (ignoring ' a ' and ' the '). Titles in foreign languages are included in the same alphabetical sequence, *eg*:

Agricultural economics research 631.105

Annales de physiologie végétale 581.105

Deutsche Landwirtschaft 630.6145

Estudos agronomicos 630.5

Journal of animal science 636.06

Journal of the British grassland society 633.205

Revue agricole de France 630.5

The catalogue card shows how far back the library's set of each periodical goes; sometimes it goes back to the very first issue of the journal, but not always. If the student has a reference to an article in the volume of a periodical published, say, in 1951, it is possible for him to tell from the catalogue, without going to the shelves, whether or not the 1951 volume is in the library's stock.'

It will be necessary to go more precisely into the uses of specific abstracting and indexing journals with science students, but humanities and social science students might at this early stage be introduced to any indexing journals easily available to them and easy to use, *eg*:

'As a subject guide to individual articles in periodicals the student will find it useful to consult the volumes of the *British humanities index* (formerly the *Subject index to periodicals*) and the *Social sciences and humanities index* (formerly the *International index to periodicals*); the sets of both these indexes are kept on shelves 73 to 75 in the main hall of the library.'

USING THE LITERATURE

An introduction to the concept of what is usually called ' the structure of the literature ' provides for science students what amounts to a map of the country in which they may spend a great deal of time in the future. A first glimpse of it could take something of the following form, passing from the idea of textbooks, with which they are familiar, to other forms of scientific publication, each with its own definite role to play within the total coverage of the records of science:

' The structure of the literature of science and agriculture
The first acquaintance students make with the literature of
science and agriculture is in the form of textbooks, but because
of the speed of development in scientific investigation, general
textbooks cannot keep pace with the most recent advances, and
they are, of necessity, somewhat out-of-date by the time they are
actually on sale in the bookshops. Since this difficulty does not
apply in the same way to periodicals, papers on recent work in
any field of science appear first of all in the top-level scientific
journals, especially those published by the learned societies
concerned with that branch of science in which the new work
has been done. These journals are the ' primary publications '
of science and agriculture; examples are:

Agronomy journal
Biochemical journal
British journal of nutrition
Hilgardia
Journal of the science of food and agriculture (including
abstracts).

As there are more than 30,000 scientific periodicals in many
languages being published all over the world at the present
time, it is obviously a difficult task for the individual scientist
to keep abreast of new advances in even a comparatively limited
field. Helps in the form of the ' secondary publications ' of
science have gradually been devised to fit his needs. These
secondary publications give, for example, reviews of the present
state of knowledge in some special field, abstracts of important
recent papers in some branch of science or agriculture, and lists
of titles of books and papers that enable the reader to keep
aware of work currently going on. Some examples in these three
categories are:

Reviews and surveys
Advances in agronomy
Annual review of biochemistry
Biological reviews
Nutrition reviews

Some of the reviews appear in book form, such as the volume edited by John Thomas Abrams and entitled *Recent advances in animal nutrition,* which appeared in 1966.

Abstract journals

An abstract is a summary of an article in a periodical (sometimes of a separate publication) accompanied by sufficient bibliographical information to enable the original article to be traced. There are journals entirely devoted to abstracts of current papers in certain fields of science, *eg*

Biological abstracts

Dairy science abstracts

Field crop abstracts

Horticultural abstracts

These last three abstract journals are just examples of the many published by the Commonwealth Agricultural Bureaux, Farnham Royal, covering animal breeding, plant breeding, soils and fertilizers, weeds, etc. A full list of the publications of the Commonwealth Agricultural Bureaux is kept at the enquiry desk in the main hall.

Lists and current bibliographies

Bibliography of agriculture

FAO library list of recent accessions

Quarterly bulletin of the International association of agricultural librarians and documentalists.

The agriculture student will also need to keep in touch with government research work and with regulations, recommendations and bibliographies issued for farmers. Some useful examples of these are:

GREAT BRITAIN. *Agricultural research council*

A bibliography of farm building research . . . (in progress)

GREAT BRITAIN. *Medical research council*

The composition of foods; by R A McCance and E M Widdowson. 3rd edn, London, HMSO, 1960 (Special report series no 297)

GREAT BRITAIN. *Soil survey research board*

Memoirs . . . (in progress)

GREAT BRITAIN. *Statutory publications office*
  Agriculture. The fertilizers and feeding stuffs regulations,
    1960. London, HMSO, 1960. Statutory instrument, 1960,
    no 1165).

Details of these are given on the cards in the Author Catalogue; it may be worthwhile repeating here that government
publications are catalogued under the official name of the
country publishing them, and in the case of this country the
name used is ' Great Britain ' not ' United Kingdom '.'

At a more advanced level a great deal more will have to be
imparted about individual abstracting journals, but most of it
will come from actually using, say, *Chemical abstracts* and *Biological abstracts* at any level up to that of a full literature search
by the research student. Other science students need to be
introduced to current awareness journals, possibly in this way:
  ' *Current awareness journals*
  There is an obvious time lag before a paper can be abstracted
  in one of the abstract journals, but lists of the titles of current
  papers can be brought out very quickly. This is done in, *eg*
    Current papers in physics
    Current chemical papers
    Current contents: life sciences.'

Even the beginner can be told of the existence of the great
Handbücher, although it will be a long time before he tackles
Beilstein or Gmelin.

As so many guides to the literature of various branches of
science have recently appeared, the student might also be introduced at least to the existence of such helps (for a list, p 88*ff*)
which may one day be of great assistance to him. The instructor
is imparting instruction not only for the present, but also for
the future when the student becomes a teacher and must keep
up-to-date, does research and must find out about the researches
of others, or else works in industry and must be able to cope
with problems not included in his university courses.

The skeleton structure of the literature of the social sciences
and the humanities is not as clearly discernible as that of the

pure sciences, but for the purposes of reader instruction the bibliographic organization is the important element, and most subjects exhibit the basic distinction between primary and secondary sources. Compared with science, the weakest section of the bibliographic organization in the humanities is that of abstract journals; there is nothing resembling *Chemical abstracts*. The following is a suggestion for a rough basic list of categories of material that can be adapted to many disciplines:

Primary sources

Artifacts, historical MSS, works of art, literary texts, maps, archives.

Secondary sources

Monographs, papers on primary sources, source books, *Corpora*, accounts of expeditions, theses and dissertations.

Third hand material

Proceedings of societies, reports of conferences.

Works of synthesis: textbooks, histories.

Media giving approach to other material

Past:

Guides to records and archives

Encyclopedias

Dictionaries

Lexicons

Handbooks

Bibliographies

Catalogues

Biographies and collected biographies

Calendars

Current:

Abstract journals (*eg Bulletin signalétique: sciences humaines*)

Collected indexes (*eg Social sciences and humanities index*).

A librarian is often required to give elementary instruction in a subject quite new to him, but he can tackle it in the way usually followed by information officers, that is, by first reading a summary article in an encyclopedia and glancing at the pattern of the reference books and bibliographies in Walford,

Winchell, Maclès and other constant companions of his working life. Any existing ' guides to the literature ' of his new subject are obviously invaluable and must often be his greatest stay and support. The preliminary chapters in standard textbooks frequently contain excellent summaries of the field, and it is useful to look through the syllabuses for his subject in the university or college calendar, and to get acquainted with any departmental booklists or stencilled notes that he can manage to obtain. The illustrations that he chooses in this way cannot have the close relevance to the course of similar examples that would be chosen by the teaching staff in those particular weeks of the academic year, but they will enable the librarian to get somewhere near the paths the students are likely to be treading. When drawing up library exercises or projects, he will again get help from many of the ' guides to the literature ' which give lists of such exercises; otherwise he can work backwards from the publications themselves. The following are some examples of the kinds of library exercises that may be devised. If various different types of projects are handed out to the members of one class, the subsequent discussion can cover very many more points than if all do the same question. Usually one question can be framed to accomplish several allied purposes.

1 Who wrote the article on Chartism in
    (i) *Encyclopaedia Britannica* and
    (ii) *Chambers's Encyclopaedia?*
An exercise to introduce the student to the idea that there is more than one encyclopedia, to discover by reading the articles that the treatment differs, and to realize that it is possible to find out who wrote the individual articles.

2 How many editions are there in the library of Burke's essay on the sublime and beautiful? Give details.
A practical exercise to show the existence and meaning of ' editions ' and the need for care and thought in using the catalogue. The exact title of Burke's essay is deliberately not given, and the alphabetical arrangement of the titles in the catalogue separates one edition which actually uses *An essay . . .* as the

title, from editions with the full title of *A philosophical enquiry into the origin of our ideas of the sublime and beautiful;* the possibility that the text also appears in collected editions of Burke should also be investigated.

3 Are there any German translations of Virgil in the library? Which English translation of Virgil in the library is of particular literary importance? Has any research on Virgil been carried out at any time by a member of this university? What is the latest critical work on Virgil in the library?

An example of a multiple question based on one major author; it requires the student to get familiar with the arrangement of the entries under Virgil, to think about translations and the great writers who have made translations and to be aware that a scholar connected with the university in question had recently published a monograph on Virgil.

4 How far back does the library's set of the *Annual bibliography of English language and literature* go? Compare it with the *Year's work in English studies* and make a list of i) three similarities; ii) three differences.

An exercise in finding in the catalogue and in handling and examining with careful attention these two standard serial works whose titles sound very similar.

5 How would you begin to look in the library's catalogues for Smith's *Dictionary of modern English literature?*

Designed to warn students of the difficulties of finding books by 'Smith' (unless they have the forenames) in the catalogue of a large library in the English speaking world; it is also designed to lead to searching the subject catalogues under several possible headings.

6 By what society is the *Journal of linguistics* published? Are there any names familiar to you on its editorial board?

An exercise in the closer examination of periodicals to judge their authority and standing. Obviously the student in the university concerned will find the names of some of his teachers on the editorial board.

7 Imagine you are a student of sculpture visiting Lucca.

(i) Using the appropriate volume of Touring Club Italiana:

Attraverso l'Italia as a guide, find out which two Renaissance sculptors are well represented in the town.

(ii) Using the library's subject catalogues, try to find more information about these sculptors and better illustrations of their work.

A wider question with the future in mind, designed not only to induce the student to start off from the known to the un-known in the library, but to bring home to him that such self-help in holiday planning holds possibilities for the rest of his life. A few students respond to such questions with enthusiasm.

8 What books i) by David Hume ii) about David Hume were published in Great Britain in 1964? Give details of authors, titles and publishers. Have we copies in the library?

A straightforward question, first in the use of the *British national bibliography,* then in precision in noting down authors, titles and publishers, and finally in the necessary step of consulting the library's own catalogues.

9 Are the library's books on the subject of Utilitarianism found in more than one place on the shelves? If so, where are these other places and with which subjects are the books classified?

Using only the library's catalogue, find which of these books contain a bibliography and how long each biblio-graphy is.

Which of the library's major encyclopedias has the longest article, and which the fullest bibliography on Utilitarian-ism?

A different type of multiple question from the one on Virgil, using a fairly narrow subject as the basis. It involves thinking about the reasons for different placings in the library and the classification scheme, using the library's catalogue to find out about bibliographies and to judge their length from the pagina-tion given there, and also using different encyclopedias and discovering that some may have very useful bibliographies.

10 Give the full titles of the following journals, of which the abbreviations given are those used in the *World list of*

scientific periodicals:

Advmt. Sci., Br. Ass.

C.r. hebd. Séanc. Acad. Sci., Paris

Chem. Ber.

Mh. Chem.

Q. Rev. chem. Soc.

Which of these journals is in the library and how long is the run in each case?

If any are not in the library, which is the nearest library that takes them?

A straightforward exercise in the use of the *World list* and the *British union catalogue of periodicals,* and the library's periodicals catalogue, introducing a method of locating journals that will need to be used frequently in the student's future.

11 A conference on the education of professional physicists was held in London in 1965. There is a report of this conference in the library. Fill in a reserve slip for it.

Designed to give practice in finding reports of conferences in the catalogue, and in filling in reserve slips with the correct heading when the author is not a personal one.

If the questions have been set some time ago, or repeated from a previous session, it is essential that the books, periodicals, abstract journals to be used should actually be handled by the instructor himself before the time of the seminar, so that he should still have the feel of them in his mind. It is almost inevitable that if the teacher neglects this first-hand check, the periodical in question will have chosen that very issue to announce its cessation, the abstracts journal will that month cancel one of its long established supplements, or the yearbook will recently have changed its name and divided itself into two.

LIBRARY AND INFORMATION NETWORKS

For a complete picture of the resources that he can tap in his search for information, the advanced student needs to have some idea of the facilities outside his own library that are available to him. A rather distorted notion of the purposes of inter-library loans is sometimes given when students are told in their first week that they can get ' anything they want through other libraries ', but for research students inter-library loans and special information networks can be of vital importance.

It is not necessary here to sketch in this background either for Britain or for other countries, except possibly to suggest that the pattern might be traced as covering an ever-widening area from the local region to the national and international areas. Against such a background of general library provision and co-operation, the networks of specialized subject coverage can be described, including recent computerized special information services like MEDLARS, UKCIS, INSPEC, and so forth. Possibly some indication of what is involved in drawing up profiles for such computerized services might also be given.

Since with so great an undertaking as the supply of scientific information international co-operation is essential, and since this may loom increasingly large in the future of those who are students now, time might be found for some mention of UNISIST, the Joint UNESCO-ICSU (International Council of Scientific Unions) project in the communication of scientific information and the feasibility of a world science information system. At the moment six working groups are busy on such subjects as indexing and classification, bibliographic descriptions and language problems, and there is an advisory panel of representatives of MEDLARS, INSPEC, EURATOM, and the American Chemical Society. One of its proposals concerns a machine file of periodical titles and standard serial numbers on the analogy of the standard book numbers to which libraries have swiftly grown accustomed. Several regional centres will be selected as pilot projects, and these would act as clearing houses for publications and focal points for the exploitation of duplicate magnetic tapes of information stores; they would also act as centres not only for the training of information staff but for information users.

The photographic copying services of all kinds that are available in the individual or national information centres are again obvious topics. The librarian would be well advised to include explanations and warnings about breaches of copyright and what may be regarded as fair copying, to use the Royal Society's expression.

OTHER AIDS: WRITING DISSERTATIONS, PUBLICATION, ASKING FOR INFORMATION

Questions of copyright often lead logically to problems about preparing dissertations, publishing, proof reading, the citation of references, and so on. All librarians know of published guides to these matters and many libraries have drawn up lists of those in their own stock. The organization of personal indexes, the handling of peek-a-boo cards and so on can also be touched upon, although unless the instructor is himself an expert in the subject of the reader's research, he can only confine his assistance to general principles and would be ill-advised to embark on the construction of anything very elaborate.

Requests for very detailed and expert assistance are likely to increase with the growing practice of appointing information officers to the staff of university libraries. The time may come when an individual officer may have to draw a strict line between instructing or advising a student and actually doing his bibliographical searches for him. Academic information officers can seldom act as personal research assistants, as they sometimes do in industry, and there is the additional factor to be considered that part of the purpose of a student's course is that he should be learning how to use the literature for himself, and part of the value of a well-documented doctoral thesis lies in the fact that the candidate has found his own material and recorded it acceptably, so that he may, in his turn, guide his own advanced students when he comes to act as supervisor to them.

Fortunately academic libraries are not greatly plagued with 'mugwumps', who, according to Carl H Kraeling, are readers who are already suffering from indigestion of facts and should be discouraged from gorging themselves with more, but academic information officers may sometimes have to formulate priorities for work which is piling up.

One of the most useful contributions a librarian can make to the smooth working of all information services is to teach enquirers how to ask for information. There are three easy rules that can be imparted with profit to all concerned:

1 Enquiries should be as specific as possible, *eg*, do not ask for ' everything you have about power stations ', when really what you want is material on acidity in transformer oil.

2 Enquirers should give an indication of the purpose for which the information is needed. This is not to encourage idle curiosity in the mind of the information officer, but to give him the correct level for his searches; *eg*, material on Palladian houses in southern Britain for a paper to be read to a society on the history of architecture, will be different from that needed to prepare a talk for school children on an outing to Chiswick House.

3 Enquirers should say whether they have already looked for material themselves, and, if they have, be more specific about it than ' I have looked everywhere '. Much waste of time is avoided by their giving precise information about exactly which libraries, which reference books, which abstract journals, etc, have already been tapped and with what results.

5
Case histories—microbiology I

However many books and articles may be written setting out syllabuses for reader instruction, they cannot be a substitute for experience of the actual teaching situation. To sit-in on another instructor's class is more enlightening for the beginner, but this is often difficult to arrange and a certain amount of constraint is sometimes introduced by the presence of a visitor. The writer believes that if teachers describe their teaching experience as honestly as they can, this effort at sharing can be particularly valuable in the present experimental stages of library instruction, and, in this belief, the following chapters of this book will be devoted to 'case histories', describing seminars covering several different subjects conducted for students at several different levels. They do not give a complete cross-section of every kind of reader instruction at all possible levels, but they do cover a wider field than usual and so enable a more comprehensive view to be taken. As the classes were all conducted by the same person, there is similarity of purpose in the teaching underlying the variety of subjects taught.

The first case history describes seminars given to microbiology students in the last term of their first year at the university, the second, in chapter 6, describes seminars and talks to typography students in their second and third years, and the third, in chapter 7, recounts experiences in seminars for postgraduate students in English and in food science. The university at which the classes were given was the University of Reading in Berkshire, England, with a student population of some 5,000, where library instruction was first begun in 1965.

In order to increase the impact of what are 'real life situations', the case histories are written in the first person and sometimes in the present tense.

In January and February 1971 I gave a short course of three library instruction seminars to microbiology students. It was a repetition, with adjustments, of a course I had given in 1970, which had originally arisen from a request for such a course made by two lecturers in the Department of Microbiology, Dr P and Dr T. They had made it quite clear that the request was not an official departmental one, since they could not truthfully say that all their colleagues were convinced of the necessity for library instruction, but they themselves felt their own students would benefit from such tuition and they would be glad if I would arrange to do it. I gladly consented and I received from them every assistance and friendly support.

In my preliminary discussions with Dr T and Dr P, I was anxious to get as clear an idea as possible of what they felt their students needed to be taught at this stage of their course and I planned the contents of my seminars against this background. I learnt that the students were in the last term of their first year and had just decided to take microbiology as their major subject. Although first-year students, one or two had worked in industrial or medical laboratories for a while. During their first two terms no books had been definitely recommended, but the lecturers provided me with a stencilled list of eighteen reference books in microbiology, chemistry and biochemistry, held either in the main university library or the Department of Microbiology's own small library; these were the books they felt their students would benefit from learning to use. They also drew up fifteen exercises or projects on the pattern of similar types of questions drawn up for students in the Faculty of Agriculture (see below p 80) which they had seen. I was most grateful that they had agreed to do this, since their questions would be focussed on topics of genuine concern to their students. Specialists though they were, they found the task of formulating such questions more difficult than they had expected. They kindly added notes about likely sources for my own benefit, and when I worked through all the projects in detail before the seminars, I used these notes as my main guide to sources, supplementing them with other sources that occurred to me. As is normally the case when I prepare for a new subject, after my own preparatory reading I found microbiology absorbing and even for a time regretted I had not elected to become a microbiologist.

The seminars took place during a lull of six weeks before the students were to write their first university examination; the 1971 seminars ended earlier than their 1970 predecessors, because I had found that the cloud of the imminent examinations had overshadowed student interest at the end of the 1970 course. Timetable arrangements, including notices, encouragement and reminders to students, were carried out by Dr T and Dr P. This was important, because the seminars were not part of the required syllabus. The series consisted of three weekly seminars arranged for four small groups—three groups of 5, and one group of 4 students—19 students in all. I met one group at 10 am for about an hour, followed by a coffee break; then another group at 11.30 for a seminar with the same basic content. I repeated the whole process with the remaining two groups during the second three weeks. Although this may appear a rather wearisome arrangement, I prefer to teach small groups, as I find the increased personal contact more satisfactory; my actual teaching varies with the response of the students and I adjust to this as I go along; my jokes (or what I hope are jokes) are not repeated from class to class.

The venue was one of the microbiology laboratories in a hut on the university's old site, about half a mile from the main university library. We sat in a little group in one of the gangways between the benches, with background noises from apparatus which could not all be switched off, even temporarily. To the students this atmosphere was familiar; to me it was exciting, if initially distracting.

The books I actually used in the seminars were either borrowed from Dr T's personal collection in his office, or from the departmental library. The only publication I took with me was a specimen issue of *Biological abstracts,* which had been withdrawn from the main library as being slightly defective and passed to me to make what use of it I could.

FIRST SEMINAR

Every student has a copy of the printed *Library handbook* when he comes to the university and can be assumed to know that it gives hours of opening of the main library, plans, and library rules. At the first seminar, I, as it were, supplement this by giving out copies of the lists of reference books prepared by Dr T and Dr P, and copies of a stencilled *Introduction to the university library for students in the Faculty of Science,* which I wrote to take the place of information I used to impart in a preliminary talk. It covers the following topics:

1 Arrangement of the Main Library
2 Catalogues
    2.1 The author catalogue
    2.2 The subject catalogues
    2.3 The periodicals catalogue
3 The structure of the literature of science
4 Guides to the literature of science
5 Reference books in the main hall

(Inside cover—definitions of ' periodical ', ' pamphlet ', ' abstract '.)

I tell the students that I shall take this as read and digested before the next seminar, and as it is quite brief (7 pp) and they see some value in reading it before next week, most of them do so.

I briefly begin the first seminar by explaining what we are trying to do in our three meetings together in what is still an experiment in the best way to help them. I outline what value their lecturers and I hope the course will have for them both during their university career and after graduation when they do research, or perhaps go into a public health laboratory or into industry. I also explain that I shall give them each a project to work on before the next seminar, making it quite clear that the project has been devised by Dr P and Dr T and that, although I am not a scientist, I have worked through all the projects myself and have survived.

I supplement the *Introduction to the university library for students in the Faculty of Science* by pointing out sections they might find particularly useful before they begin their projects, and I also say something about the different places in Dewey in which they, as microbiology students, will find their books, *eg*

Microbiology	576

but also

Medical Sciences	610
Medical Microbiology	610.01
Bacteriology	589.9
Mycology	589.2
Biology	574
Microscopy	578

I also go through the list of reference books. Few of them have yet bought any books themselves, but if they have, we discuss them, especially if they can be used as information sources.

At some convenient stage I hand out the projects, a different one to each student. The ones chosen for this seminar entail the use of reference books. I give three examples:

Find two recipes for tris buffer, pH 8.0, ionic strength 0.05, from two different sources.

What is ' Köhler illumination ' in microscopy and under what circumstances is it used?

The Therapeutic Substances Act (1965) refers to the potency and purity of antibiotics, amongst other substances. What organism is recommended for the biological assay of penicillin?

I take great pains to explain that these are not examination questions, but exercises designed to supple the mind to think about the literature of science, and to learn to use it by actually using it. Only time tells whether the students really accept this, as they are so accustomed to questions being ' tests ', and they do not invariably credit my insistence that the exercise is just as valuable if they do not as if they do find the information asked for, provided they do their best, and make the necessary precise notes about their search, step by step. Some are helped by the suggestion that they should try to imagine for themselves a situation in their future career in which they might need the information asked for.

Some find it easier to work with another student when they do their searching, and I make it clear that this is acceptable since they should work in the way that suits them best.

At this first seminar we actually handle one or two reference books, perhaps the *British pharmacopoeia* as there is a copy near. We spend a little time examining its arrangement, scrutinizing the title-page for evidence of date and the status of all concerned with its publication, commenting on the value of prefaces, and relating it to the *Extra pharmacopoeia* and the *British pharmaceutical codex*. They have never assessed a book in this way before.

The actual order in which I deal with each section of the seminar varies, as I find such changes offset for me the fact that I repeat each seminar four times during the six weeks; basically the content remains the same but the comments vary quite widely.

As the students will be rather lost about the way to begin working on an actual problem, I usually end the first seminar by analysing some questions which they have not had given them, but which are yet somewhat similar to theirs. To take one from Bottle and Wyatt's *The use of biological literature* serves the added purposes of telling them about that book and letting them see that such exercises are not just a diabolical invention never heard of elsewhere. Two such questions are:

Name suitable test organisms for the biological assays of penicillin, streptomycin and polymixin.

Give alternative names for the following organisms: *Escherichia coli. Salmonella typhi. Staphylococcus aureus, Bacillus globigii, Micrococcus lysodeikticus*.

The analysis consists of breaking down an enquiry into parts and asking what kind of publication might be expected to contain the answer to each part; we work through their list of reference books, and discuss *exactly* how we would track down the actual books in the main library, of which they have had little first-hand experience. We also discuss how we might use any particular volume—contents list, index, alphabetical arrangement, etc. It gives some of them confidence if I tell them in some detail exactly what *I* do when I start working on an information query, step by step from the main hall of the library to the catalogue, the shelves, and so on. I also tell them that they may well find the information in other places than those to which their lecturers and I directed our search, and indeed they frequently do. The whole enterprise is intended to be flexible, and this is stressed because it is necessary that information work should be taught against the background of a real situation.

SECOND SEMINAR

At the beginning of the second seminar I ask whether the students have any questions on the *Introduction to the . . . Library,* partly as a means of reminding them to read it.

We then go through their experiences in handling the exercises. I found that the previous analysis of another question at the first seminar (I only started this in 1971) seems to provide them with the kind of guidance that is necessary, and very few of them are completely unsuccessful. We discuss each step of their search in detail so that I am able to share their experience, make suggestions as to what else they might have done at certain stages and often to applaud their own ingenuity. This is partly done to familiarize them with the whole atmosphere of information searching in a definite library on a definite day when the book one had hoped would be on the shelf is—quite legitimately—being used by someone else; the situation must be accepted and, where possible, circumvented by approaching other publications. This not only helps the students to be resourceful, but also illuminates the fact that a library is used by many people, none of whom has exclusive proprietary rights over its contents.

These discussions take some time. If one of the students who took a question has not turned up at the second seminar, I go through his project with the rest of the class, asking for suggestions from them as well as going through my own notes on it. After this I hand out new questions, trying to assign the slightly more difficult ones to those who have shown the most ingenuity in their first effort. The new questions include those requiring the use of periodicals; the following are three examples:

Briefly summarize the advantages of the scanning electron microscope for examining Actinomycetes which were reported in the *Journal of general microbiology* about three years ago.

A more sophisticated method for examining the bacterial surface has recently been described. It is the scanning electron microscope. The first successful commercial instrument was described in both *New scientist* and *Science journal*. Consult one of these descriptions and give the principles of the instrument.

Early attempts at sectioning bacteria and examining them under the electron microscope were not successful. Early satisfactory results are recorded in a paper by Chapman and Hillier (1965). Give the full reference to the paper, the name of the organism studied and the substance of the findings with regard to the way in which the cell cross walls are formed.

I point out to the students that these questions concern scientific periodicals, and use this as a stepping stone to explain that we are now working at the other extreme of the structure of the literature of science, the frontiers of new knowledge, in contrast with standard textbooks, reference books, encyclopedias, handbooks, etc. The students have read the outline of this in the *Introduction* but I enlarge upon it. I introduce the idea of a periodical, getting this as clear as possible; if pressed, the students will usually produce the titles of a couple of popular non-scientific magazines, or perhaps the *New scientist,* but few have even heard of *Nature.* I expound the magnitude of the problem of control of the number of scientific periodicals and scientific papers published, using the latest figures

I can find. As I myself found John Ziman's *Public knowledge* very interesting, I pass on to them the picture it gives of the scientific consensus and the practice of refereeing scientific papers.

Dr T has told me that he would like these students to have some acquaintance with four core journals at this stage, and I have with me the current (or nearly current) issues of them, which I now introduce to the class:

Journal of general microbiology
Journal of applied bacteriology
Journal of bacteriology
Bacteriological reviews

Two of these journals have particular connections with both the department or the neighbourhood and the special interests of the university; there is much to say about this, leading to the more practical examination of the actual issues of the journals I have brought with me—their status as the organs of scientific societies, periodicity, etc. The differences between the British and the American journals can also be pointed out. The location of bound volumes with indexes and any cumulated indexes can follow next.

We then turn to specific papers in the journals, the affiliations of the authors, the authors' abstracts, the date the MS was received, and directions to contributors, and anything that occurs to me as we look at the issue together. Then, as it has been agreed with Dr P that the students should learn how to set out references at the end of papers and essays, we examine what their major journal, the *Journal of general microbiology*, does in this respect, pointing out the purpose of references as validating the claims made in the paper. Actually it had, at the time of my 1970 seminar, asked authors to stop abbreviating journal titles in references, as the 'abbreviations are now becoming so bizarre that many are a nuisance to trace'. This leads us to examine what information is actually necessary and why it is necessary, differences that are basic or differences that are only typographical house rules, etc. If there is time, I get the students to write references as for the end of their own as yet non-

61

existent essays for certain papers in these journals. One or two stumble over this, mainly through finding the conventions finicky, but they soon learn to accept them. Also if there is time I point out that *Bacteriological reviews* is in a slightly different category from the other three, and this will lead me to review journals and abstracts next week.

THIRD SEMINAR

Discussing the second batch of projects takes up the first part of the third seminar. Most students find the transition from books to periodicals a bigger step than it looked, and the scientific information explosion takes on a little more reality for them.

This last seminar I devote to talking about, handing round and exploring some of the contents of review journals and other surveys of the state of the science, abstract journals and current awareness journals. As suggested, the examination of *Bacteriological reviews* as one of their core journals has given me the opportunity to show the characteristics of reviews, and leads me to mention other *Advances, Annual reviews* and *Progresses* in the field.

The main university library does not take *Microbiology abstracts,* Section A (Industrial Microbiology) and B (General Microbiology and Bacteriology), but I am able to borrow copies from the departmental library, so that the class can look at them in detail. I also take along my specimen issue of *Biological abstracts* and am able to spend some time showing the extent of the coverage ($\pm$ 8,000 serials in nearly 100 countries) and the arrangement, analysing individual abstracts to discover author affiliations, full titles of cited journals, original language, etc. For a few abstracts, we trace the course that must be taken to find the original article, either in the university library or in another British library holding the copy. This last only introduces them to the idea of a network of co-operating libraries in the country, which, later in their career, should have more meaning for them. I also introduce the existence of a KWIC index.

Finally, I touch briefly on current contents or current awareness journals and how they are compiled. When the time comes, the students will at least have heard of them, and they are thus brought to the end of the ' control of the literature ' line along traditional methods. If the occasion arises in a particular class I mention experiments in computerized information retrieval.

RETROSPECTIVE THOUGHTS

What do I believe, or hope, has been accomplished by such a course in reader instruction? I had asked Dr T to let me have any reactions from students after the previous course, which he kindly did, and they were favourable but general, so the only analysis I can offer is my own:

1 Fruitful co-operation between library and departmental staff was established.

2 The students were led into the literature of science first in the familiar surroundings of their own laboratory and then on their own two feet into the main library, where they had some success in searches that had some meaning for them.

3 They gained some acquaintance with the structure of the literature of science and the differences between the categories of scientific publications.

4 They got to know and use certain specific publications in their own specialty which their teachers were sure they needed to know.

5 They actually handled reference books, periodicals and abstracts, and learnt what to look for and how to appraise them from bibliographical evidence.

6 They learnt the necessity for care and precision in using bibliographical language and in setting out references.

7 They learnt how to tackle an information problem by analysing it and proceeding step by step from the known to the unknown, in an effort to solve it.

8 They were introduced to the scientific consensus and to the existence of the checks that validate an individual scientist's work, only possible when it is published.

9 They thought about their own future and related ' the world of recorded knowledge to the world of living people '.

6

Case histories—typography II & III

My work with the university's Typography Unit, one of the sub-divisions of the Department of Fine Art, is an example of the way reader instruction grows naturally out of different contacts and adjusts itself to changing needs and circumstances. Typography has been a personal interest of mine since the days when I worked at the Nonesuch Press, and I lectured to librarianship students on modern book production at the University of the Witwatersrand in South Africa. So although I am no typographer, I was naturally glad to be asked three years ago by Dr M T, the head of the unit, to talk to his third year students (see below, p 67).

Out of these yearly talks and out of a couple of information queries in the field of typography that I worked upon last year, it was arranged that Dr M T and I should hold two library instruction seminars for his post-first-university examination students in June 1970. These students had recently taken their first university examination and were set for their courses in Typography; they were, therefore, actually first year students in the last few weeks of their first session, but in effect already second year students waiting to begin work in their special subject.

The brief course was based on two classes separated by fifteen days to fit in with everyone's timetable commitments. The entire year (8 students together with Dr M T himself) took part. Dr M T and I discussed beforehand what topics might be introduced. The students were already users of the library but they needed to understand it better and to be able to find information for themselves. As a result of our talks, Dr M T provided 16 questions on information projects, and a list of 28 bibliographies and other works of reference on which (after consultation with him) I marked those eight he considered most important for the students to get to know about at this stage. I also received first-year booklists on a) theory and practice of typography and b) history of typography, a long second-year booklist, and a list of 29 current periodicals with asterisks for four of them considered 'most important for undergraduates'. I then worked through the first six questions, all I had time for, making notes about how and where I found the information, about false trails, and any other possible sources to tap. These six questions were:

1 How many editions were there of Senefelder's treatise on lithography? List them and give the dates and places of publication.

2 Give the author and title of three English printing manuals of the nineteenth century.

3 Who was Frank Pick?

4 When were the following published:

J Tischold	:	*Die neue Typographie*
J D Harding	:	*The park and the forest*
Baskerville's		*Bible*
J Moxon	:	*Mechanick exercises*
P Dupont	:	*Essais pratiques d'imprimérie*

Before the class I sent to the unit enough copies of my stencilled *Introduction* for each student to have one; most of them would have had a copy previously, but they might have lost it and/or not read it; I told them I would assume that they had all digested the contents. I have already quoted from the three versions of this booklet for letters, science and agriculture students, but may repeat here that its contents, very simple, cover the following topics which would be the basis from which we began our discussions:

1 Arrangement of the library
2 Catalogues
    2.1 The author catalogue
    2.2 The subject catalogues
    2.3 The periodicals catalogue
3 Guides to books on selected subjects

3

4 Reference books in the main hall.

The classes were held in my very small office in the library that just allowed everyone to sit on a chair. The talks were quite informal but guided by myself.

I had gathered from odd remarks that this year's typography students were particularly worried about the classification scheme and the fact that their books were dispersed among widely separated classification numbers. I made available to them copies of Dewey's Second Summary Divisions and I also put up on the wall an enlargement of the first page of the full tables of 655 : Printing, Publishing, Bookbinding, with its handy summary and its enlightening instructions to the classifier:

For prints and print making	See 760
„ book illustration	„ 741.64
„ value and influence of the book	„ 002
„ bibliography	„ 010
„ music printing and publishing	„ 781.98

This brought home to them, in a way they could understand, the actual alternatives confronting the classifiers. We went through the advice about placings in some detail and they seemed to realize better the linkages in an overall classification scheme, with its advantages as well as disadvantages. I also put up on the board enlarged detailed schedules for 655.2 and we discussed such recent changes as machine composition, now at 655.28, and hand composition, now at 655.25.

I talked about reference books, bibliographies, abstract journals, etc, as illustrated by their lists; I stressed the importance of the title page to the cataloguer as well as the typographer, and tried to find out exactly how those of the group who had used the main university library actually went about finding what they needed. This is always a probing analysis and not without humour. Armed with some knowledge of the kind of approach they were making, I made suggestions about other steps that might be taken and indicated how one tackled information problems by analysing what one needed to find out and the kind of publication that might be expected to be the likeliest quarry for it. Then each one present (or group of two if they wished it) was given a different problem from Dr M T's list, with a fortnight in which to find the information needed.

At the second class we went through each information search in great detail, including the false trails followed at certain stages; first the student recounted what he had done and then I made any additional suggestions that I could. Of equal value to the experience of the search is the training in using bibliographical terms precisely and in recording *exactly* which periodical was looked at, how far back in a set a vain trail went, and so on. The combination of the students' more specialized knowledge of typography (*eg* about Senefelder) and my own longer experience of information searches (*eg* looking for translations in foreign library catalogues) resulted in a wider view of the possible information sources for each project. Dr M T's highly expert knowledge made the searches range even more widely into some fascinating tracks, and added excitement to the chase for material which was obviously of genuine interest to the class.

The two seminars seemed to Dr M T and myself to have served a useful purpose, although we decided that in 1972 they should be transferred to early in the autumn term of the students' second year. This will avoid the distraction of the long vacation.

TYPOGRAPHY III

This talk was given as a result of a request from Dr M T to the university librarian in 1968 that he should give a lecture to the typography design students on the function of university libraries and information services, in a series intended to alert the students to the needs of print users in an age of computers, xerox machines, microrecords, etc. Members of the staffs of the psychology, linguistics and applied physical sciences departments were to take part in the series. The university librarian passed the request on to me. I was glad to comply, but I was vague as to what contribution I could usefully make, and after some consultation with Dr M T, I decided to give what I thought might be relevant, and hope for the best. The range of what I essayed can best be conveyed from the following notes used for my talk, which I called:

'INFORMATION STORAGE AND RETRIEVAL: TRADITION AND EVOLUTION

Storage and retrieval-computer language an old problem for libraries. The printed book and its offspring, the periodical, not the only form but certainly the handiest. Old forms—Egyptian temple archives (papyrus and skin)—Assurbanipal's clay tablets—Alexandria—roll books, medieval monasteries—MS codices on vellum.

Books themselves arranged in many ways—sizes, authors, contents of books, *ie* knowledge—classified by a systematic order and logical system. Science—Aristotle's method. Age of reason and systematization (Linnaeus, Haller). Oxbridge college libraries, gentlemen's libraries, mechanics institutes, self-help, public libraries.

Melvil Dewey; Library of Congress; Bliss; Ranganathan PMEST.

Problems of contents: double subjects, misleading titles.

Science/technology information explosion. Control journals (abstracts, surveys, current awareness, etc). Royal Society Information Conference. Classification Research Group. Rapid retrieval—punched cards, computers. International co-operation; coverage by separate subject; MEDLARS, etc.

For printers—Printing abstracts; collective indexes. Changes in forms—microfilms, microcards, microfiches, xerox, data transmission devices, audio-visual aids. Present pattern of libraries in Britain and USA.'

I spoke for an hour to Dr M T and his third year students; the reception was interesting and lively. From the questions I realized that the history of the book from the clay tablet to paperback was familiar ground, so that when I was asked to repeat the talk in 1970 I omitted most of this, but added more material on work being done by the British Standards Institution on the treatment of documents, and by iso/tc 46 on documentation standards; they were interested in a librarian's point of view on this.

The us National Advisory Commission on Libraries *Recommendations* had recently come to my attention, and I took *Libraries at large* to the class with me, reading out the main proposals and parts of the section on ' Future directions in library operations and services '. As typographers, the students were particularly interested in the paragraphs on ' The role of books and other media ' (p 324), as any great changes will affect them even more than librarians—a fact that librarians seldom consider.

When the time came for the talk to be given a third time (1971), I completely changed the content, partly for variety and partly because I had just returned from a computerized information retrieval training course in Oxford, and wanted to tell them about this. I therefore started with this course as an actual example of how a computerized information retrieval service works, told them what the training course had covered and showed them actual profiles and computer print-outs, which they had never seen. They had already had a talk from a lecturer in the Department of Applied Physical Sciences, so the foundation was laid for me to recount my first-hand experience. The fact that this service provided a current awareness print-out service from data bases confined to *Chemical titles* and *Chemical-biological activities* of *Chemical abstracts,* pin-pointed the fact that even international computerized services are at present covering only sections of knowledge, however important, and that the press-button access to all knowledge is still a long way off. This gave me a lead to turn from this most recent activity in the field to say a word about others (MEDLARS, INSPEC), and then to make the leap backwards in time to summarize the history of previous efforts at classification, spending more time on faceted classifications and on Ranganathan than I had up to this year.

7
Case histories—postgraduate seminars

The two case histories in this chapter are examples of two different types of seminars for postgraduate students: the first describes a group of three seminars for students beginning work for their MA and PHD degrees in English literature, and the second describes a single but repeated introductory seminar for postgraduate students in food science.

ENGLISH

An American professor in the Department of English asked the university librarian to arrange for some bibliographical guidance to be given to the department's postgraduate students at the beginning of their first session of research, and I undertook to give this guidance. The little course was intended for six students, although not all of them came to all three seminars. One was a Dutch student who had not yet used the university library, but the rest had used it during their undergraduate years. Three of the students had as yet not made up their minds about the subject of their research, three had decided to work respectively on Edward Thomas, Hazlitt and verse published in eighteenth century periodicals.

I therefore decided that the course should be called ' Bibliographical tools of research in English literature ', but seminar I was angled on tools for research into the work of a twentieth century English poet; seminar II—research into essays of the Romantic Period, and seminar III—research into eighteenth century periodicals and minor poetry. This allowed me to take three different but connected approaches to the bibliography of English literature; the choice of the most recent period as the initial one gave me the chance to include recent and general bibliographies first and to work backwards from them; the undecided students could then spend their time getting to know the general bibliographies while they were still making up their minds about their particular topics. Each of the three seminars led on from the more general previous one and each student received copies of all three rather detailed annotated booklists that I prepared.

SEMINAR I

The booklist for this seminar was arranged under the following headings:

Search on a 20th century English poet

A Handbooks for students of English (such as Bond's *Reference guide to English studies*).

B National library catalogues; national bibliographies; books in print.

C Subject bibliographies.

D Annual surveys and bibliographies.

E Indexes to periodicals; modern collected indexes.

F Guides, lists and abstracts of theses.

At their first seminar, which lasted about an hour, I explained the meaning of bibliography within the present context, and pointed out the usefulness of having an idea of the map of the entire bibliographical countryside before embarking on a particular journey. I gave hints about first using material near at hand, mentioning certain special collections in the university library itself and spending a litle time on the classification, and on headings in the subject catalogue that might have been overlooked. I then talked about establishing which was the standard text (to be decided in consultation with their supervisor), and about the usefulness of any existing bibliography of a writer as a starting point, with examples.

Finally I worked through my stencilled booklist in very considerable detail. This gave the opportunity of discussing where they would be able to see material not in the university library and the best way of tracing articles in journals, finding the location of the journals in BUCOP, xerox-copies, and so on.

During the subsequent year I sent any relevant newspaper cuttings or publishers' leaflets to the student working on Edward Thomas, and she came to see me a few times about bibliographical difficulties she had encountered. I naturally was very careful never to usurp her supervisor's position and responsibilities, and only to supplement his guidance with bibliographical information.

SEMINAR II

The booklist for seminar II was arranged as follows:

Search based on an essayist of the Romantic Period

A Standard text and standard bibliography.

B Bibliographies covering the period.

C Surveys of research on the Romantics.

D Guides and indexes to contemporary periodicals, including finding lists.

E Bibliography of bibliographies and guides to reference books.

At the actual seminar, after referring to the sections from last week that led to this, I talked about this era of the Great Reviews and recent work on them. Hazlitt's interest in Shakespeare, the stage, Malthus, cultural and intellectual history, style, art and contemporary politics gave me the opportunity to suggest ways of using more general guides to reference books to cover these interests. I also introduced a little information about cancels (suggested by Sir Geoffrey Keynes's *Bibliography*), copyright, the new Wellesley index and nineteenth century ' literary anecdotes '. I mentioned the usefulness of chronological tables of happenings in the years when Hazlitt lived. These topics were suggested rather than thoroughly discussed, because such discussion was not my task; but pointing out further ways to supplementary information did fall within my province.

SEMINAR III

The booklist for seminar III covered:

Search based on poetry in 18th century periodicals

A Bibliographies.

B Lists of poetry.

C Studies and lists of periodicals.

D Provincial periodicals.

E Special collections, ' Illustrations ', etc.

As I had examined nearly all the publications afresh for this seminar, I was able to point out certain entries in them which might lead along a useful trail. This seminar also logically included studies of the periodical press, of burlesque poetry, topographical poetry, nature poetry, chapbooks, garlands, and finally of publishers like Dodsley.

The arrival of a handsome and timely bookseller's catalogue from Dublin, with a long and detailed section on English verse 1700-1800, gave me the opportunity to mention such sources and examine some of their fascinations.

RETROSPECTIVE THOUGHTS

I found that, in spite of my own experience of research in English literature, the preparation I needed to do for these three seminars was very considerable and, of course, it had to be precise and to be checked to the last detail. Most of the time I was in the dark with regard to any precise knowledge of the work each student was actually engaged upon at the time, and I am inclined to think the whole exercise would have been more effective as a purely departmental one, for which I would most willingly, however, have drawn up all necessary lists, consulting with the supervisor about them and handing them over to him to discuss with his students.

Personally I did not find the seminars as intellectually stimulating as I usually do when I am working in a new subject field, and this threw some light for me on the fact that subject specialists often find the bibliography of their own subject rather boring and are disinclined to spend the necessary time on it for the guidance of their students.

There are also certain special perplexities to be faced by the librarian who teaches postgraduate students on his own, with little guidance from the department. Is he just to treat the matter as he would for a class in bibliography, or is he to focus more definitely on the students' specialist requirements? The responsibility for supervising the thesis is not, of course, his, and it is professionally obligatory for him to refrain from interfering or disturbing in any way the relationship between student and supervisor, and on occasion the student may try to use his contact with the librarian to grumble about his supervisor. This is comparatively easy to sidestep.

A more subtle difficulty is that of a current departmental viewpoint on a subject. An obvious example is the field of English literature with its ' new criticism ', close analysis, literary history, sociology of literature, and other approaches. Nearly every university department denies that it has a departmental viewpoint and insists that the student must judge for himself, but in practice the impartiality is difficult to maintain; there may indeed be rival camps in one department. The librarian must obviously be even more scrupulously impartial, although he would naturally find it extremely helpful to know the affiliations of the department, if only to avoid misunderstandings.

Even without having experience of research himself, a librarian over the years acquires considerable knowledge of the information-gathering habits of postgraduate students, and this he should apply to give the seminars the necessary contact with actual individual situations which the printed guides must lack.

One requirement of the conductor of the seminar is adjustment to differing backgrounds of students with degrees from other universities or from other countries. The latter sometimes encounter language barriers at the beginning of their courses, the time they usually come for library instruction, but the help it is possible for a library to give a postgraduate student cannot include substantial instruction in the language of the university he is currently attending. The librarian must also remember that the student is there partly to get acquainted with research methods, so that if he finds he is being too freely used as a research assistant to one student, this may defeat one of the purposes of a postgraduate course.

At the initial stage the exact limits of the field in which the student will write his thesis are almost invariably vague, and he will need to range in a far wider area than the one to which he finally limits his study.

FOOD SCIENCE

Students coming to Britain from all over the world for post-graduate work often have special difficulties. Problems of language and differing backgrounds obviously spring to mind, but others only reveal themselves in the course of contact with individuals or groups. The following case history may bring out some of the ways in which librarians can help.

A lecturer in the Food Science Department on Reading University's London Road site telephoned me to ask whether I could give library instruction to some overseas students doing postgraduate work in food science. This was all the information I had and I did not meet the lecturer himself.

There were a couple of false starts, because of messages not getting through, one of the hazards of a divided university campus, and even more hazardous in the case of overseas students new to the idea of library instruction. Finally, in the middle of their second term at the university—that is, after most of them had had some experience in using the library, but no formal introduction to it—I arranged to give one seminar (repeated three times) to a group small enough to meet in my own office on the science floor of the main library. The seminars were attended by 7, 4 and 6 students respectively (17 in all). There was one English student among them, but the rest came from Nigeria (3), Pakistan (3), Iran (1), Ceylon (1), Iraq (2), Thailand (1), Venezuela (1), India (1), Turkey (1), Malaysia (1), Sudan (1). They were many years older than British MSC students, and some held very responsible posts in their own countries.

They had already received the printed *Library handbook* and *A select bibliography and library guide to the literature of food science* prepared by a member of the staff of the department in 1969. I myself prepared for them (January 1971) an 8-page stencilled list of *Research in food science: some useful bibliographical tools,* arranging the entries in the following categories and

75

giving the university library's call numbers when we had copies:

1 Bibliographies.
2 Surveys and ' recent advances '.
3 Abstracting, indexing and current contents journals.
4 Guides to writing papers and theses.

In drawing up this list I made it as full as possible, including as much as I could on bibliographies of agriculture in tropical and sub-tropical countries (*eg*, an Indian agricultural bibliography), or in languages other than English (*eg*, *Bulletin signalétique: section 380*, and *Landbouw-documentatie*) and international sources (FAO references and Commonwealth Agricultural Bureaux publications). My annotations to the abstracting journals, which I later explained, showed the connections from the present *Food science abstracts* back through its various predecessors, to help them if they wished to make a full literature search.

On the blackboard I put down the various Dewey numbers they might find it useful to remember, in addition to food technology and general food books at 664, *eg* 612.3 nutrition, 613.2 calorie tables, 543.1 chemical analysis, and the various main and subdivisions of subject headings and ' see also ' references they might handle in the subject catalogues (alphabetical subject-cards) and the agricultural pamphlets catalogue, a sheaf catalogue with different subject headings.

I also made available copies of the *Introduction to the . . . Library* for undergraduates in the Faculty of Science and the Faculty of Agriculture, since the subject falls into both faculties, and I could talk both about the structure of the literature of science and of agriculture and know that they had a reminder at their disposal.

Language was a considerable problem, but I spoke as clearly as I could and soon got used to the many different accents. The difficulty of using bibliographical terms precisely, experienced with all students, is obviously considerably increased with such a multiplicity of mother tongues.

The pattern of each seminar was the same. Initially I found out their names and where they came from—there was much

76

friendly hilarity over the names—and some idea of what they were going to use their degrees for when they got home. Quite a number were particularly interested in dairy science, which led me to tell them a little about the National Institute for Research in Dairying and its close connections with the university.

I then enquired about difficulties in the library and how they found material in the library, probing in some detail. Difficulties in finding individual books could only be handled by referring them to the enquiry desk, but basically their problems hinged on not being used to a large library, and their having discovered that the search for material is more demanding than they had presupposed. They also lacked experience of handling books as tools.

I then went through the stencilled list in detail. I based my approach on the structure of the literature of science, explaining and stressing the references likely to be of use to them when they return home. They were quite unused to abstracts, unless some felt it polite to *say* they were unused to them—I could not quite decide.

I had fetched a bound volume of *Nutrition abstracts*, with its useful review articles, from the reference shelves and we examined it in some detail, tracing a few abstracts back to the finding of the original articles, and confronting the problem of language, in which they were, of course, particularly concerned. My ever-useful copy of *Biological abstracts* was called into play as an example of a major abstracting journal, and it provided at least a preliminary view of a KWIC index. There was only time to refer to the existence of *Dairy science abstracts*.

We packed as much as possible into the one seminar of 50 minutes, and the atmosphere was pleasant and animated—more animated than with British students. Their main difficulty was language, including the necessity for writing papers in English. I had included several aids for writing dissertations in my booklist, but they still hoped for a few words of direction from me that might enable them to write, say, like Bertrand Russell. I trust that it helped them to find that each in his own way had the same fundamental difficulties. Strangely enough, it cheered them to know how many of the tools are in English, and that the painful acquisition of a world language has its unexpected uses. Their seriousness of purpose and their courtesy was a refreshment to me and the slight feeling of constraint when one cannot tell whether one's words are being fully understood can always be offset by a positively friendly manner.

There is a good case for individual ' walkie-talkie ' introductions to the library for overseas students, but where possible the human approach in one brief seminar is needed to supplement this.

The holding of an actual seminar, specially arranged by their department, with names of people attending formally sent in to the instructor, served to emphasize the importance of the literary background to more advanced scientific work, not always stressed in their scientific world overseas, and the introduction to the idea of a structure of scientific literature reinforced this importance.

8
Some other methods of instruction

Although currently much emphasis is laid on producing audio-visual aids to assist students to improve their use of books, traditionally it has been other books, either in print or near-print, that have been brought into service for this purpose, as, for instance, the published guides to the use of Beilstein by Huntress and by Richter and Ilberg. Certainly the book, as a form, is extremely convenient. Leaflets and stencilled hand-outs are only a subdivision of this same linear approach to learning upon which our book-built educational system has for so long been based. These hand-outs and leaflets proliferate in library instruction circles, and most librarians are willing to make them freely available to colleagues, either by gift or exchange, and they are often listed in annual reports or library handbooks. They vary greatly in size and scope: three taken at random from a pile of such compilations are:

' *Whitaker's almanack* '—Edinburgh College of Commerce
Library

2 stencilled pages (1 sheet)
Facts about publisher and date, the kinds of information covered and the arrangement of the index.

How to find out: a brief guide for arts students
Southampton University Library
Folder of 4 pages
Covers: Finding a book in the catalogues; finding material on a subject; finding information on a subject; finding out what reference books to use; using the library staff.

Gmelin's handbook of inorganic chemistry
University of Surrey Library
(Information sheet 1) 3 p and 2 tables

Introduction; Classification scheme; Table of contents and indexes; Future.

2 tables (Gmelin system of elements and compounds; Coverage of the elements).

Rather more closely connected with organized reader instruction are booklets of 'exercises' in using the library. These can be used in conjunction with classes, or as exercises for the students to do on their own with the encouragement of their departmental tutors. In at least one case an 'answer book' is also issued separately, not for the use of the student but of his tutors; answers obviously afford a useful opportunity for an explanation to the tutors of the purpose behind each question, not always visible at the first glance. The complete booklet in question listed 24 literature-of-agriculture questions, sub-divided into subject sections matching the departments in the agricultural faculty of the university. Two examples will suffice to indicate the treatment; in each example the first part is quoted from the students' question booklet and the second from the tutors' answer booklet:

Question (Horticulture):

If you are given a reference to horticultural abstract no 4274 of 1960 as the summary of an article on colour in hydrangeas, could you trace in the library the original article so that you could read the complete text?

Answer:

The student should first look up *Horticultural abstracts* in the periodicals catalogue, arranged alphabetically by title. He will find the classification number to be 634.05 and will see that the library possesses the volume for 1960. When he goes to the shelf he will find that the actual abstracts are consecutively numbered in each yearly volume, and that no 4274 of 1960 is ASEN, Sam. A rapid method for evaluating the colour of *Hydrangea macrophylla* sepals. *Proc. Amer. Soc. Hort. Sci.*, 1959, 74: 677-80 (=Proceedings of the American Society of Horticultural Science). The student must then consult the periodicals catalogue again, looking under *Proceeding of the American Society of Horticultural Science.* He will find that the library has a set of this which includes vol 74 (there are, in fact, *two* volumes per calendar year), and he will find this volume on the shelf at 634.06, and be able to read the original article in full.

Question (Agricultural botany):
Steward's *Plants at work* lists three useful sources in which the status of selected botanical topics is reviewed from time to time. Are these sources in the library, and if so, how far back do the library's sets go, and what is their classification number?
Answer:
The first step is to find Steward's *Plants at work.* From the author catalogue one finds that the library has a copy of the 1964 edition at 581.1 in the main collection. There is also a copy in the reading room. At the end of his selected references, on p 180, Steward lists the three sources as *Annual review of plant physiology, Botanical review* and *Symposia of the Society for the Study of Growth and Development.*

The next step is to look in the periodicals catalogue arranged alphabetically by the first word of the title. From this the following information can be obtained. One complication is that the periodicals catalogue uses the singular ' Symposium ' instead of the plural ' Symposia ' as the filing word in the last item.

Annual review of plant physiology
The library has from v 1, 1950 onwards   class no 581.105
Botanical review
The library has from v 1, 1935 onwards   class no 580.5
Symposium of the Society for the Study of Growth and Development
The library has 11th, 13th, 16th, 17th to 22nd   class no 574.13
The last is an example of an incomplete run; a library does not necessarily always possess a complete run of a periodical or serial publication.

Other methods of promoting the better use of libraries are quizzes, essay competitions with book-tokens as prizes, discussion panels and teach-ins. These are outside the main structure of reader instruction, but they can have a real value in themselves in addition to that of publicising the library.

At the level of spreading understanding of methods of searching for information, an ingenious idea was recently worked out at Southampton University Library, in its ' Crown of Thorns ' (Acanthaster Planci) project, when several departments of the university, as well as the library, co-operated in a search for information to help towards the solution of a genuine problem facing the Great Barrier Reef in Australia. The wide ramifications of such an information search could be made vividly manifest.

Such schemes are ambitious and demand a greater investment of effort than every library can afford to expend. The trouble with brilliant ideas is that it is difficult to repeat them at the same level.

In some circles the danger has been recognized of students' essays being based on the contents of the same few well-thumbed recommended books, even in institutions where the library's resources go well beyond such a minimum. Two years ago an experiment to induce wider reading was undertaken in connection with a course on contemporary France. Two lecturers in the French Studies Department and the Bibliographical Consultant on the library staff collaborated to produce a reading list of some size (55 pages), subdivided as follows:

1 General works. Geography and environment including culture.

2 Political history, up to and including the Fourth Republic.

3 Political history, the Fifth Republic.

4 Constitution and administration, central and local.

5 Political Parties.

6 Foreign affairs, the end of Empire, the Army and Defence since 1940.

7 Economic history and conditions since 1945.

8 Interest groups, Employers' associations, trades unions, etc.

9 Social classes and groups, women, intellectuals, technocrats, etc.

10 Religion.

11 Education and communications media.

12 Periodicals and yearbooks.

The lecturers chose the titles from a large selection of slips tracked down in the library by the Bibliographical Consultant; theirs was the decision as to inclusion or omission, but the consultant supplied expertise to make the list bibliographically acceptable. It is difficult to judge whether improvement in students' essays was attributable to this list, but the venture was successful enough for a new edition to be prepared late in 1971. The consultant was careful not to attempt to judge the contents of the books listed, nor to make the decisions about relevance (except in the reference section), believing very firmly that evaluation in such cases is the province of the students' own teachers.

The field for collaboration in compiling reading lists of this kind is wide open and can only lead to fuller and more accurate lists and to improvement in the students' angle of vision on the library's coverage of his subject.

Tutor-librarians, having responsibilities both for subject teaching and the library, do not need to observe such scrupulous professional etiquette. For example, the stencilled sheets recently handed out by a college of commerce library in Britain include not only lists of works of reference, and information about the catalogues and subject index, but other material nearer in approach and content to teaching-notes for seminars in English literature, *ie*, ' Why read a novel ' (notes on William Golding's *Lord of the flies*), and ' Why read a play ' (notes on Arthur Miller's *Death of a salesman*); these notes give some analysis of the text, followed by comments and questions suitable for English literature discussion groups.

9
The future

Apart from the work of tutor-librarians, reader instruction as at present interpreted remains largely instructional rather than educational, and emphasizes the value of the library as a storehouse of knowledge rather than a storehouse of wisdom and understanding; it may thus be thought to reinforce a utilitarian approach to university education, with an increasing concentration on the acquisition of vocational qualifications rather than on the enrichment of the personality. This dismays those librarians who have based their faith in libraries on a belief in their value as treasuries of the great thoughts of master spirits, embalmed and treasured for successive generations. These librarians have regarded their own work as a contribution to the conservation and enrichment of their collections. to be handed on to the future. They wonder whether this view of libraries, which gave them the strength and vision for their own calling, still has any meaning in the educational world of today; if it has lost its appeal, is it intrinsically so valuable that it should at all costs be revived?

Another recent social trend affecting libraries has been the popularity of group ' happenings ' that involve ' togetherness ' and sound—poetry reading, pop festivals, teach-ins, record-playing sessions, constant radio background. Will this continue, or will the need for the therapy of peace and of periods of solitude for the health of the personality re-assert itself? Ironically enough, constant music played in college halls of residence has, in certain places, sent many students back to the library in order to find peace and quiet for study.

Reading has of late been subject to some censure as a sterile, selfish occupation. Should some librarians still hold to their belief that people *need* to read for personal enrichment as well as information, that the printed text of a poem, although fixed and permanent, does not grow stale but may mean different things at different times, even to the same reader who returns to it; that reading and quiet response is a way to a wider and deeper understanding of life? And should not the library world believe, as Don Lacy suggests, that the library can provide the specific complement to the power of the mass media, with their dispensation of instant wisdom and ill-considered judgments, because the book is ' our one major communication device that deals with an audience as individuals, and communicators as a collection, and so reverses the typical pattern of communication of our generation '.

The many statistical surveys of the use of libraries by present-day students offer little help to those anxious to take a wide and long view, and to plan not just for tomorrow but for the far future. The statistics have been gathered over a comparatively narrow field during a short span of time, and that span of time forms only part of a period of unprecedented increases in numbers of students and of changes in their motivation, attitudes and habits. It would surely be imprudent to extrapolate from such results and to base comprehensive future plans upon trends yet only currently and dimly discerned. After the upheaval and the protest, where are the growing points to be found, and how can abiding values be upheld in the flux?

Can the libraries, for instance, do anything to span the increasing gaps between academic subjects; can they be bridge-builders? Fortunately the specialization and departmentalization which have ' destroyed the general unity of scholarship ' (John Ziman's words), are deplored not only by librarians, but by many scholars with greater influence in high places; yet librarians feel that theirs is a special responsibility, for under their care lies a means to combat the fallacy that each department or discipline in a large modern university can honestly subsist unto itself. The ' crisis in learning ' which has recently attracted wide concern cannot be clearly seen if analysed only on a departmental basis. The librarian is in a position to see it spread over a much wider area, and this confronts him with the obligation to try to do what he can to redress the balance and to serve the very widest educational ends. Some of this work is indeed carried on by public libraries, where the pressure of examination reading weighs less heavily. Previous generations of university librarians provided browsing rooms or arranged discussions on the *Synotopicon* and the 'world's great books', but such schemes no longer match the mood of the times: browsing collections are very vulnerable to illicit 'borrowing', and immediate political and social activities, rather than 'great books', pre-occupy the students of the seventies. Even if the university librarian plans displays of his library's treasures or arranges exhibitions in connection with some special anniversary, he must, if such exhibitions are to be acceptable by modern standards of display technique, expend a considerable amount of money on professional assistance or allocate to them a disproportionate amount of his own staff's time. He may find that such occasions seem likely to become infrequent but impressive exercises in general publicity and public relations, rather than bridges connecting subjects in the university curriculum.

Projects recently launched, however, show that there is much experimentation in new ways to achieve the end of true education through books; their very diversity shows how great the problem is and how essential is co-operation both within the university and outside. For instance, Washington and Lee University in Lexington, Virginia, has embarked upon a project which 'provides for faculty and student participation in making the university community more knowledgeable about the total resources of the library system, its reference services, the relative strengths and weaknesses within disciplinary collections, and the ways to make most effective use of the resources at hand and those available through inter-library cooperation'; it is 'characterized by campus-wide cooperation'; each participating department will name a liaison professor who will teach an intensive bibliographical course dealing specifically with library resources available in the department's field, and it is hoped that eventually the programme 'may develop into a permanent university-wide system designed to integrate maximum familiarity with the library into every student's undergraduate education '.

Jackson State College is formulating ' Project LAMP ', a venture in which students, lecturers and library staff will cooperate in trying to motivate the students to explore the world of creativity beyond the limits of the syllabus, and to explore the arts and humanities through literature, philosophy, painting and sculpture, music and the theatre, Wabash College in Indiana has announced its intention to seek to change the concept of the library from that of a storehouse of information to that of a workshop of the liberal arts, and to give the student the opportunity of seeing what the intellectual life can be like by ' living it along with the professor '. Much may emerge, too, from the experiments with ' orientation librarians ' at, for example, Western Michigan University; these librarians will endeavour to provide a more personalized approach to specific bibliographical resources, and otherwise work toward a close library/faculty/student relationship. All these are experiments in the field of reader instruction in the sense that it has been used in this book, and the experience that inspired them has been obviously similar to what has been described here in different terms.

Whatever the future shape of libraries, even if many of them become multi-media storage banks of information, they must surely be designed to serve ' adequately-conceived human ends '. It is to be hoped that these ends will be more adequately-conceived and defined when the role of libraries is seen more clearly in the emerging pattern of modern academic institutions in each country and in the world, the place of each individual institution and the part it will play in the overall educational system. Until this pattern becomes clearer the librarian must make such decisions for the present and the future as his own insight and judgment indicate.

APPENDIX
Guides to subject literature

ARRANGEMENT

GENERAL—GUIDES TO GUIDES

SCIENCE AND TECHNOLOGY

General

Agriculture

Biology

Cellulose and Textiles

Chemistry, Chemical Industries, Pharmacy

Computers

Electrical Engineering

Food and Food Industries

Geography and Geology

Mathematics, Physics, Atomic Energy, Space Science

Metallurgy and Metal Industries

Patents

Rubber and Plastic Industries

Zoology

HUMANITIES AND SOCIAL SCIENCES

General

Art

Economics, Banking and Investment, Business

Education

English Literature

History

International Affairs

Music

Philosophy and Psychology

Political Science, Parliamentary Publications, Local Government

Statistics.

GENERAL, GUIDES TO GUIDES

Chandler, George: *How to find out: a guide to sources of information*. Oxford, Pergamon, 1963.

SCIENCE AND TECHNOLOGY, INCLUDING AGRICULTURE
General

Burns, R W: Literature sources for the sciences and technologies: a bibliographical guide. *Special libraries* 53, 1962, 262-71.

Carey, R J P: *Finding and using technical information*. London, Arnold, 1966.

Fleming, T P: *Guide to the literature of science*. New York, Columbia University School of Library Science, second edition 1957.

Grogan, Denis: *Science and technology: an introduction to the literature*. London, Bingley; Hamden, Conn, Archon, 1970.

Herner, Saul: *A guide to information tools, methods and resources in science and engineering*. Washington, Herner, 1968.

Houghton, B: *Technical information sources*. London, Bingley; Hamden, Conn, Linnet, 1972.

Jenkins, F B: *Science reference sources*. Champaign, Ill., Illini Union Bookstore, fourth edition 1965.

Malinowsky, H R: *Science and engineering reference sources: a guide for students and librarians*. Rochester, NY, Libraries Unlimited, 1967.

Schutze, Gertrude: *Bibliography of guides to the S-T-M literature: scientific-technical-medical*. New York, the Author, 1958. Supplements 1963 and 1967.

Townsend, A C: Guides to scientific literature. *Journal of Documentation* 11, 1955, 73-8.

Agriculture

Blanchard, J Richard and Ostvold, H: *Literature of agricultural research*. Berkeley, University of California, 1958 (University of California Bibliographic Guides).

Harvey, Anthony P (*comp*): Agricultural research literature:

a bibliography of selected guides and periodicals. *In: Agricultural research index,* fifth edition volume 2 (1970), 957-1043.

Neal, K W: *Library guide to agriculture and horticulture.* Wilmslow, the Author, 1969.

Plumbe, W J: The bibliographical basis of agricultural research with special reference to the tropics. *Tropical agriculture,* 29 (1-3), 1952, 15-27.

Singhvi, M L and Shrimali, D S: *Reference sources in agriculture: an annotated bibliography.* Udaipur, Rajasthan College of Agriculture, 1962.

Biology

Bottle, R T and Wyatt, H V *(eds): The use of biological literature.* London, Butterworth; Hamden, Conn, Archon, 1971.

Cellulose and texiles

Hearon, W M: The literature of cellulose and related materials. *Tappi* 37, September 1954, 152A-7A.

Lemon, Hugo: *How to find out about the wool textile industry.* Oxford, Pergamon, 1968.

Chemistry, chemical industries, pharmacy

American Chemical Society: *Literature resources for chemical process industries.* Washington, ACS, 1954 (Advances in Chemistry series, no 10).

American Chemical Society: *Searching the chemical literature.* Washington, ACS, 1961.

Bottle, R T *(ed): The use of chemical literature.* London, Butterworth, second edition 1969 (Information Sources for Research and Development); Hamden, Conn, Archon.

Brown, R and Campbell, G A: *How to find out about the chemical industry.* Oxford, Pergamon, 1969.

Brunn, A L: *How to find out in pharmacy.* Oxford, Pergamon, 1969.

Burman, C R: *How to find out in chemistry.* Oxford, Pergamon, second edition 1966.

Crane, E J and others: *A guide to the literature of chemistry.* New York, Wiley, second edition 1958.

Dyson, G M: *A short guide to chemical literature*. London, Longmans, second edition 1958.

Mellon, M G: *Chemical publications, their nature and use.* New York, McGraw Hill, fourth edition 1965.

Computers

Pritchard, Alan: *A guide to computer literature*. London, Bingley; Hamden, Conn, Archon, 1969.

Electrical engineering

Burkett, J and Plumb, P: *How to find out in electrical engineering*. Oxford, Pergamon, 1967.

Food and food industries

Baker, E A and Foskett, D J: *Bibliography of food: a select international bibliography of nutrition, food and beverage technology and distribution, 1936-56.* London, Butterworth, 1958.

Bootle, V and Nailon, P: *A bibliography of hotel and catering operation.* London, New University Education, 1970.

Foskett, D J: *Food canning: a select bibliography.* second edition revised by E G Watchurst. London, Metal Box Co, 1962.

Geography and geology

Burkett, Jack *(ed)*: *Concise guide to the literature of geography*. Ealing Technical College, School of Librarianship, 1967 (ETC Occasional Publication 1 / 1967).

Pearl, R M: *Guide to geologic literature.* New York, McGraw-Hill, 1951.

Wright, J K and Platt, Elizabeth, T: *Aids to geographical research: bibliographies, atlases, gazetteers and other reference books.* New York, Columbia University Press for the American Geographical Society, second edition 1948 (AGS Research Series no 22).

Mathematics, physics, atomic energy, space science

Anthony, L J: *Sources of information on atomic energy.* Oxford, Pergamon, 1966.

Essex University Library: *Physical sciences and mathematical studies: a guide to the bibliographical and reference materials held by the library,* by B J C Wintour. Colchester, Essex University Library, second edition 1970.

Fry, B M and Mohrhardt, F E: *A guide to information sources in space science and technology.* New York, Interscience, 1963.

Parke, N G: *Guide to the literature of mathematics and physics.* New York, Dover, second edition 1958.

Pemberton, J E: *How to find out in mathematics: a guide to sources of mathematical information.* Oxford, Pergamon, second edition 1969.

Whitford, R H: *Physics literature: a reference manual.* Metuchen, NJ, Scarecrow Press, second edition 1968.

Yates, B: *How to find out about physics.* Oxford, Pergamon, 1965.

Metallurgy and metal industries

Gibson E B and Tapia, E W: *Guide to metallurgical information.* New York, Special Libraries Association, second edition 1965.

Maxwell, Robert, and Co, Ltd: *Metallurgy: (a bibliography); compiled by the staff of the Documentation and Supply Centre.* Oxford, Maxwell, 1968.

Veasey, W I: Sources of information in automobile engineering. *Aslib proceedings* 13, 1961, 167-77.

White, D: *How to find out in iron and steel.* Oxford, Pergamon, 1970.

Patents

Wild, J E: *Patents: a brief guide to the patents collection in the technical library.* Manchester Public Libraries, second edition 1966.

Rubber and plastic industries

Yescombe, E R: *Sources of information on the rubber, plastics and allied industries.* Oxford, Pergamon, 1968.

Zoology

Smith, Roger C and Painter, R H: *Guide to the literature of the zoological sciences*. Minneapolis, Burgess, seventh edition 1967.

HUMANITIES AND THE SOCIAL SCIENCES

General

Clarke, J A: *Research materials in the social sciences*. Madison, University of Wisconsin Press, 1959.

Gray, R A *(comp)*: *Serial bibliographies in the humanities and social sciences*. Ann Arbor, Pierian Press, 1969.

Guttsman, W L: The literature of the social sciences and provision for research in them. *Journal of documentation* 22 (3), 186-193.

Hale, Barbara: *The subject bibliography of the social sciences and humanities*. Oxford, Pergamon, 1970.

Hoselitz, Bert F *(ed)*: *A reader's guide to the social sciences*. Glencoe, Ill, The Free Press, 1960.

Kraeling, Carl H: The humanities: characteristics of the literature, problems of use, and bibliographic organization in the field. *In*: Shera, J H and Egan, Margaret E *(eds)*: *Bibliographic organization*. Chicago, 1951.

Lewis, P R: *The literature of the social sciences: an introductory survey and guide*. London, Library Association, 1960.

Madge, J H: *Tools of social science*. London, Longmans, 1953.

White, Carl M and others: *Sources of information in the social sciences: a guide to the literature*. Totowa, NJ, Bedminster Press, 1964.

Art

Carrick, Neville: *How to find out about the arts: a guide to the sources of information*. Oxford, Pergamon, 1965.

Chamberlain, Mary W: *Guide to art reference books*. Chicago, American Library Association, 1959.

Economics, banking and investment, business

Burgess, N: *How to find out about banking and investment.* Oxford, Pergamon, 1969.

Fletcher, J *(ed)*: *The use of economics literature.* London, Butterworth; Hamden, Conn, Archon, 1971.

Johnson, H W *(ed)*: *How to use the business library, with sources of business information.* South Western Publication, third edition 1964.

Maltby, A: *Economics & commerce: the sources of information and their organisation.* London, Bingley; Hamden, Conn, Archon, 1968.

Education

Bristow, Thelma and Holmes, Brian: *Comparative education through the literature: a bibliographic guide.* London, Butterworth; Hamden, Conn, Archon, 1968.

Foskett, D J: *How to find out: educational research.* Oxford, Pergamon, 1965.

English literature

Altick, Richard D and Wright, Andrew: *Selective bibliography for the study of English and American literature.* London, Collier-Macmillan, second edition 1963.

Bate, J: *How to find out about Shakespeare.* Oxford, Pergamon, 1968.

Bateson, F W: *A guide to English literature.* London, Longmans, second edition 1967.

Bond, Donald F *(comp)*: *A reference guide to English studies.* Chicago, University Press, 1962. A revision of *Bibliographical guide to English studies,* by Tom Pete Cross.

Chandler, George: *How to find out about literature.* Oxford, Pergamon, third edition 1968.

Thompson, James: *English studies.* London, Bingley, 1971. A revision of *The librarian and English literature.* London, Association of Assistant Librarians, 1968.

History

American Historical Association: *Guide to historical literature*. New York, Macmillan, 1966.

International affairs

Conover, Helen F: *A guide to bibliographic tools for research in foreign affairs*. Washington, Library of Congress, second edition with supplement 1958.

Mason, J B: *Research resources: annotated guide to the social sciences. Vol 1: International relations and recent history indexes, abstracts and periodicals*. Santa Barbara, Clio Press, 1968.

Music

Davies, J H: *Musicalia*. Oxford, Pergamon, second edition 1969.

Philosophy and psychology

Borchardt, D H: *How to find out in philosophy and psychology*. Oxford, Pergamon, 1968.

Elliott, C K: *A guide to the documentation of psychology*. London, Bingley; Hamden, Conn, Linnet, 1971.

Political science, parliamentary publications, local government

Ford, P and G: *A guide to Parliamentary publications: what they are, how to find them, how to use them*. Oxford, Blackwell, 1956.

Harmon, Robert B: *Political science: a bibliographical guide to the literature*. New York, Scarecrow Press, 1965.

Snape, W H: *How to find out about local government*. Oxford, Pergamon, 1969.

White, Brenda: *A sourcebook of Planning information*. London, Bingley; Hamden, Conn, Linnet, 1971.

Statistics

Harvey, Joan M: *Sources of statistics*. London, Bingley; Hamden, Conn, Linnet, second edition 1971.

Select bibliography

Abercrombie, M L Johnson: *The anatomy of judgement*: *an investigation into the processes of perception and reasoning*. Harmondsworth, Penguin Books, 1969 (Pelican book).

Adler, Mortimer J *(ed)*: *The great ideas: syntopicon*. Chicago, Encyclopaedia Britannica, 1952.

Allen, K: *Use of community college libraries*. Hamden, Conn, Linnet Books, 1971.

Alston, A M: The happy medium in library instruction at the college level. *College and research libraries,* 17, 403 (1956).

Anderson, L W: Library instruction at the University of Illinois, Chicago. *Illinois libraries,* 39, 118 (1957).

Argles, M: The work of a tutor-librarian. *Library world,* 63, 314-17 (1962).

Arnold, D V: Liberty, equality and the imagination. *Library Association record,* 71(8), August 1969, 241-243.

Asheim, Lester and others: *The humanities and the library*. Chicago, American Library Association, 1957.

Ashworth, Wilfred: The information officer in the university library. *Library Association record,* 41 (12), December 1939, 583-584.

Association of Teachers in Technical Institutions: *Use of libraries: a policy statement*. London, Library Association, 1966.

Atkins, K B: The use of the college library. *Liberal education,* (4), 1963, 28-29.

Atkinson, Frank: By due steps: programmed learning techniques and the librarian. *Library Association record,* 69(7), July 1967, 239-241.

Barnett, A N: The professor and the librarian: the view from the reference desk. *Bookmark,* 15 (2) 1962, 55-58.

Bartlett, B C: Stephens College library instruction program. *ALA bulletin,* 58, 1964, 311-314.

Bath University Library: *Experimental information officer in the social sciences. Report . . . on work carried out in 1969.* Bath, University Library, 1970.

Batty, C D: *An introduction to the Dewey decimal classification.* London, Bingley, 1965(DC16), 1967(DC17), 1971(DC18).

Benge, Ronald C: *Libraries and cultural change.* London, Bingley, 1970.

Beswick, N W: The ' library-college '—the ' true university '? *Library Association record,* 72 (4), April 1970, 148-150.

Beswick, N W: ' Library-college ' revisited. *Library Association record,* 72 (4), April 1970, 148-150.

Bonn, George S: *Training laymen in use of the library.* New Brunswick, NJ, Rutgers University, 1960 (The State of the Library Art, vol 2, part 2).

Bottle, R T: Current instruction in the use of chemical literature. *Journal of the Royal Institute of Chemistry,* 25, 1961, 173-174.

Bottle, R T: Training students to use scientific and technical information. *In: Progress in library science,* 1967, 97-115.

Branscomb, Harvie: *Teaching with books: a study of college libraries.* Chicago, Association of American Colleges, 1940.

Bristow, Thelma: A reading seminar. *Education libraries bulletin,* no 32, Summer 1968, 1-9.

Brittain, J M: *Information and its users: a review with special reference to the social sciences.* Bath, University Press and Oriel Press, 1970.

Brough, K J: *Scholar's workshop.* Urbana, University of Illinois, 1953.

Brown, C M: TV or the herded tour? *Library journal,* 90 (10) 15 May 1965, 2214-2218.

Burchard, John E: *The library's function in education.* University of Tennessee Library Lecture no 3, June 1950.

Burgess, N: The library and liberal studies. *Liberal education* 4, July 1963, 22-25.

Burgess, N: Selling the library: the work of a library tutor in a technical college. *Assistant librarian* 53 (6), June 1960, 120-122.

Burke, Redmond A: The separately housed undergraduate library versus the university library. *College and research libraries,* 31 (6), November 1970, 399-402.

Burkett, Jack: The practical element of library school teaching. *Library Association record,* 72 (6), June 1970, 232-233.

Burrell, T W: *Learn to use books and libraries: a programmed text.* London, Bingley, 1969.

Carey, R J P: Experiment in co-operative library instruction. *Library Association record,* 70 (4), April 1968, 98-99.

Carey, R J P: Library instruction in colleges and universities of Britain. *Library Association record,* 70 (3), March 1968, 66-70.

Carey, R J P: Making libraries easy to use: a systems approach. *Library Association record* 73 (7), July 1971, 132-135.

Carey, R J P: *The teaching and tutorial activities of librarians with students not training for the library profession.* Thesis for Fellowship of the Library Association, 1966.

Carey, R J P: A technical information course for engineering and science students at Hatfield College of Technology. *Library Association record,* 66 (1), 1964, 14-20.

Celoria, Francis: The archaeology of serendip. *Library Association record,* 70 (10), October 1968, 251-253.

Christie, David: Tutor-librarianship—a personal view. *SLA news,* 94, Nov-Dec 1969, 414-416.

Clemons, J E: Teaching bibliographical sources and styles to graduate students. *College and research libraries,* 17, 1956, 403.

Coblans, Herbert: Control and use of scientific information. *Nature,* 226 (5243), 25 April 1970, 319-321.

Collison, Robert L: *Library assistance to readers.* London, Crosby Lockwood, 1956.

Connor, Judith Holt: Selective dissemination of information: a review of the literature and the issues. *Library quarterly,* 37 (4), October 1967, 373-391.

Cook, Margaret Gerry: *The new library key.* New York, H W Wilson, second edition 1963.

Corney, Elizabeth: The information service in practice: an experiment at the City university library. *Journal of librarianship,* 1 (4), October 1969, 225-235.

Cowley, J: Technical college libraries: 2—Tuition in library use. *Technical education and industrial training*, 6 (9), 1964, 442-444.

Crossley, Charles: Education in literature and library use. *Library world*, 71 (839), May 1970, 340-47.

Cuming, Agnes: The organisation of a university library. *Library Association record*, 28 (1), January 1926, 129.

Davies, I R: The dual role of the tutor-librarian. *Teacher in Wales*, 5, 1965, 1-3.

Davis, R A and Bailey, C A: *Bibliography of use studies*. Philadelphia, Drexel Institute of Technology, 1964.

Deale, H V: Our responsibilities to the college undergraduate. *ALA bulletin*, 56, 1959, 500-502.

Dean, E Barbara: Television in the service of the library. *Library Association record*, 71 (2), February 1969, 36-38.

Engelbart, Douglas C: Special considerations of the individual as a user, generator and retriever of information. *American documentation*, 12 (2), April 1961, 121-125.

Enright, B J: The university library: key to education and communication. *Quest*, 4 March 1969, 7.

Erickson, E W: Library instruction in the freshman orientation program. *College and research libraries*, 10, 1949, 445.

Escarpit, Robert: *The book revolution*. London, Harrap, Paris, Unesco, 1966.

Fagerburg, D S: Future teachers learn to use the library. *Library journal*, 84, 1959, 2574.

Foskett, A C: *A guide to personal indexes, using edge-notched and peek-a-boo cards*. London, Bingley, second edition 1970.

Foskett, D J: *Assistance to readers in lending libraries*. London, James Clarke, 1952.

Foskett, D J: The intellectual and social challenge of the library service. *Library Association record*, 70 (12), December 1968, 305-309.

Foskett, D J: The library in the age of Leisure. *Library Association record* 69 (1), January 1967, 7-10.

Freiser, L H: Information retrieval for students. *Library journal*, 88, 1963, 1121-1123.

Fussler, Herman and Simon, Julian: *Patterns in the use of books in large research libraries*. Chicago, University of Chicago Press, second edition, 1969.

Gates, Mrs Jean (Key): *Guide to the use of books and libraries*. New York, McGraw-Hill, second edition 1969.

Gee, Ralph D: Algorithmic mathematical reinforcement: the implications of programmed instruction for the librarian. *Library Association record*, 67 (7), July 1965, 228-232.

Genung, Harriett: Can machines teach the use of the library? *College and research libraries*, 28 (1), January 1967, 25-30.

Gore, D: Anachronistic wizard: the college reference librarian. *Library journal*, 89, 1954, 1688.

Great Britain: Committee on Higher Education: *Higher education: report of the committee appointed by the prime minister under the chairmanship of Lord Robbins, 1961-63*. London, HMSO, 1963-4 (Cmnd 2154) 7 vols.

Great Britain: Department of Education and Science: *A plan for polytechnics and other colleges: higher education in the further education system*. London, HMSO, 1966 (Cmnd 3006).

Great Britain: Department of Education and Science: *The use of books*. London, HMSO, 1964.

Great Britain: Office for Scientific and Technical Information: *Students' chemical information project. Final report*. London, OSTI, 1969, 2 parts.

Great Britain: University Grants Committee: *Report of the Committee on Libraries*. London, HMSO, 1967 (The Parry report).

Great Britain: *Report of Committee on University Teaching Methods*. London, HMSO, 1964 (The Hale report).

Griffin, L W and Clarke, J A: Orientation and instruction of the graduate student by university libraries: a survey. *College and research libraries*, 19, 1958, 451-4.

Gwynn, S E: The college library at the University of Chicago. *College and research libraries*, 14, July 1953, 267-268.

Gwynn, S E: The liberal arts function of the university library. *Library quarterly*, 24, 1954, 311.

Hale, Sir Edward: Library and undergraduate: 1. The Hale Committee report. *Library Association record,* 68 (10) October 1966, 355-357.

Hartz, F R: Freshman library orientation. *College and research libraries,* 26(3), May 1965, 227-231.

Hatt, Frank: A day in the life of a tutor-librarian. *Assistant librarian,* 60(3), March 1967, 38.

Hatt, Frank: My kind of library-tutoring. *Library Association record,* 70 (10), October 1968, 258-259.

Havard-Williams, P: The student and the university library. *Library Association record,* 60 (9), September 1958, 269-272.

Havard-Williams, P: The teaching function of the university library. *Universities review,* 30, 1958, 61.

Havard-Williams, P and Dovey, L A: Reader instruction in Commonwealth university libraries. *Library Association record,* 62, 1960, 10-13.

Hepworth, Philip: *Assistance to readers.* London, Association of Assistant Librarians, 1951.

Hertel, R R and others: TV library instruction. *Library journal,* 86 (1961), 42.

Holley, E G and Oram, R W: University library orientation by TV. *College and research libraries,* 23 (6), 1962, 485-491.

Hunt, K E: *Collecting, storing and using information.* Oxford, Institute for Research in Agricultural Economics, 1962.

Hunt, O R: Where is the general reference librarian and bread-and-butter service? *College and research libraries,* 26(4), 1965, 307-10, 326.

Hutchinson, Ann: Films and filmstrips on librarianship and related subjects. *Library Association library and information bulletin* no 10, 1970, 7-26.

Hutton, R S: Instruction in library use: a needed addition to the university curriculum. *Proceedings of the 17th Annual Conference of Aslib, 1942.*

Hutton, R S: Training students in the use of libraries. *Universities quarterly,* 4, August 1950, 389-92.

The IDEXICON, *a guide to the great ideas of the Eastern and Western worlds,* New York, Crowell-Collier, 1961.

Jackson, W Vernon: The interpretation of public services. *Library trends,* 3, 1954, 188.

Job, D E: The tutor-librarian course at Garnett Training College for Technical Teachers. *Library Association record,* 66 (4), 1964, 167-169.

Jolley, L: The function of the university library. *Journal of documentation,* 18, 1962, 133.

Johnston, J F: The college librarian's work with students. *Education libraries bulletin,* 21, Autumn 1964, 1-21.

Josey, E J: The role of the college library staff in instruction in the use of the library. *College and research libraries,* 23 (6), 1962, 492-498.

Kennedy, James R: Integrated library instruction. *Library journal,* 95 (8), 15 April 1970, 1450-1453.

Knapp, Patricia B: *College teaching and the college library.* Chicago, American Library Association, 1959 (ACRL monograph no 23).

Knapp, Patricia B: *Experiment in co-ordination between teaching and library staff for changing student use of university library resources.* Detroit, Wayne State University, 1964.

Knapp, Patricia B: The library as a way of excellence in education. *ALA bulletin,* 57, 1963, 1039.

Knapp, Patricia B: The meaning of the Monteith College library program for library education. *Journal of education for librarianship,* 6, 1965, 117.

Knapp, Patricia B: Methodology and results of the Monteith pilot project. *Library trends,* 13 (1), 1964, 84-102.

Knapp, Patricia B: *The Monteith College library experiment.* New York: Scarecrow Press, 1966.

Knapp, Patricia B: The Monteith library project: an experiment in library-college relationship. *College and research libraries,* 22 (5), 1961, 355-362.

Knapp, Patricia B: The role of the library in college teaching. *Bookmark* (Idaho), 16 (1), 1963, 7-11.

Knapp, Patricia B: A suggested program of college instruction in the use of the library. *Library quarterly,* 26, July 1956, 224-31.

Knight, Douglas M and Nourse, E Shapley *(eds)*: *Libraries at large: tradition, innovation, and the national interest*. New York, Bowker, 1969.

Lewis, May Genevieve: Library orientation for Asian college students. *College and research libraries*, 30 (3) May 1969, 267-272.

Library Association: University and Research Section: Working party on instruction in the use of libraries and in bibliography at the universities. Report. *Library Association record*, 51, 1949, 149-150.

Linden, Ronald: *Books and libraries: a guide for students*. London, Cassell, 1965.

Line, Maurice B: *The college student and the library*. Southampton, University Institute of Education, 1965.

Line, Maurice B: Information services in academic libraries. *IATUL proceedings* 5 (1), May 1970, 28-34.

Line, Maurice B: Information services in university libraries. *Journal of librarianship*, 1 (4), October 1969, 211-224.

Line, Maurice B: University libraries and the information needs of the researcher, a provider's view. *Aslib proceedings*, 18, 1966, 178.

Line, Maurice B and Tidmarsh, Mavis: Student attitudes in the university library: a second survey at Southampton University. *Journal of documentation*, 22, 1966, 123.

McComb, R W: Closed circuit television in a library orientation program. *College and research libraries*, 19, 1958, 387.

Mackenna, R O: Instruction in the use of libraries: a university library problem. *Journal of documentation*, 11 (2), June 1955, 65-72.

Mackenzie, A Graham: Reader instruction in modern universities. *Aslib proceedings*, 21 (7), July 1969, 271-278.

Melum, V V: Library instruction to 2,000 freshmen. *College and research libraries*, 21 (6), November 1960, 462-468.

Mews, Hazel: Library instruction concerns people. *Library Association record*, 72 (1), January 1970, 8-10.

Mews, Hazel: Library instruction to students at the University of Reading. *Education libraries bulletin,* 32, Summer 1968, 24-34.

Mews, Hazel: Teaching the use of books and libraries, with particular reference to academic libraries (Chapter 14c, *British librarianship and information science, 1966-70.* London, Library Association). (In the press.)

National Council for Educational Technology: *Higher education learning programmes information service.* Catalogue of materials available for exchange, London, NCET, 1971.

O'Reilly, Shirley: Reader education (1): a readers' advisor's programme. *Australian academic and research libraries,* 1 (1), Autumn 1970, 16-20.

Owen, Edith M: Closed circuit television in the library. *Education libraries bulletin,* 27, Autumn 1966, 24-27.

Page, B S and McCarthy, S A: Library provision for undergraduates. *College and research libraries,* 26 (3), 1965, 219-224.

Page, B S and Tucker, P E: The Nuffield pilot survey of library use in the University of Leeds. *Journal of documentation,* 15, (1959), 1.

Parry, Thomas: University libraries and the future. *Library Association record,* 70 (9), September 1968, 225-229.

Perkins, R: *Prospective teachers' knowledge of library fundamentals.* New York, Scarecrow Press, 1965.

Phipps, B H: Library instruction for the undergraduate. *College and research libraries,* September 1968.

Plumb, J H (ed): *Crisis in the humanities.* Harmondsworth, Penguin, 1964. (Pelican book.)

Poole, J B: Information services for the Commons: a computer experiment. *Parliamentary affairs,* 22 (2), Spring 1969, 161-169.

Postlewaite, S: *An audio-visual approach to learning, through independent study and integrated experience.* Minneapolis, Burgess, second edition 1969.

Power, Ellen: Instruction in the use of books and libraries. *Libri,* 14 (3), 1964, 253-263.

Pritchard, Hugh: Pre-arrival library instruction for college students. *College and research libraries,* 26 (4), 1965, 321.

Pugh, L C: Library instruction programmes for undergraduates, historical development and current practice. *Library world,* 71 (837), March 1970, 267-273.

Reid-Smith, E R: The use of books and libraries by students in a college of physical education. *Education libraries bulletin,* 24, 1965, 1-14.

Revill, D H: Teaching methods in the library: a survey from the educational point of view. *Library world,* 71 (836), February 1970, 243-249.

Richnell, D T: The Hale Committee report and instruction in the use of libraries. *Library Association record,* 68, 1966, 357-361.

Robinson, Eric E: Developments in higher education and their implications for libraries. *Library Association record,* 71 (5), May 1969, 142-143.

Rooker, Margaret: Tools and tactics, the framework for an experiment in introducing students to the college library. *Education libraries bulletin,* 22, 1965, 29-41.

Rothstein, S: Reference service: the new dimension in librarianship. *College and research libraries,* 22 (1), 1961, 11-18.

Royal Society: *The Royal Society scientific information conference ... report and papers submitted.* London, Royal Society, 1948.

Rzasa, Philip V and Moriarty, John H: The types and needs of academic library users. *College and research libraries,* 31 (6), November 1970, 403-409.

Saunders, W L: Humanistic institution or information factory? *Journal of librarianship,* 1 (4), October 1969, 195-209.

Saunders, W L: *University and research library studies.* Oxford, Pergamon, 1968.

Schiller, A R: Reference service: instruction or information? *Library quarterly,* 35, 1965, 52-60.

Sellers, R Z: What shall we do for freshmen? *Wilson library bulletin,* 24 January 1950, 360-365.

Sewell, P H: Technical college libraries: developments and needs ... *Library Association record,* 68 (12), December 1966, 423-427.

Seyer, Brian: The tutor librarian. *In: Progress in library science 1965,* 192-194.

Sheehan, Helen: The library-college idea; trend of the future? *Library trends,* 18 (1), July 1969, 93-102.

Shera, Jesse H: The quiet stir of thought or, what the computer cannot do. *Library Association record,* 72 (2), February 1970, 27-42.

Shores, Louis: The undergraduate and his library. *University of Tennessee Library Lectures* 11, 1961, 25-36.

Shores, Louis, Jordan, Robert and Harvey, John: *The library-college,* Philadelphia, Drexel Press, 1966.

Siefker, B: Programmed instruction on the use of the card catalog. *Southeastern librarian,* 12, Fall 1962, 149-152.

Silberman, Charles: *Crisis in the classroom, the remaking of American education.* New York, Random House, 1970.

Slater, M: *Technical libraries: users and their demands.* London, Aslib, 1964.

Society for Research into Higher Education: *Research into library services in higher education.* London, SRHE, 1968.

Southern Illinois University: *Educational media research center. A study to determine the extent to which instruction to university freshmen in the use of the university library can be turned over to teaching machines.* Carbondale, Southern Illinois University, 1963.

Stanford, Edward B: Residence hall libraries and their educational potential. *College and research libraries,* 30, May 1969, 197-203.

Standing Conference on National and University Libraries (SCONUL). *Seminar on human aspects of library instruction, 9th December 1969, held at the University of Reading.* Proceedings. Cardiff, SCONUL, 1970.

Stone, C Walter: The library function redefined. *Library trends,* 16 (2), October 1967. (Special issue: Library uses of new media of communication).

Stone, E O: The encouragement of reading. *College and research libraries,* 22 (5), 1961, 355-362.

Student use of libraries: an inquiry into needs of students, libraries and the education process. Chicago, American Library Association, 1964.

Sullivan, Peggy (ed): *Realization: the final report of the Knapp School Libraries Project.* Chicago, American Library Association, 1968.

Swank, R C: The educational function of the university library. *Library trends,* 1, 1952, 37.

Taylor, R S: A coordinated program of library instruction. *College and research libraries,* 18, July 1957, 303-306.

Tidmarsh, Mavis N: Instruction in the use of academic libraries. *In:* Saunders, W L (ed): *University and research library studies.* Oxford, Pergamon, 1968, 39-83.

TV library instruction, symposium. *Library journal,* 86 (1), 1961, 42-46.

Urquhart, D J: Developing user independence. *Aslib proceedings,* 18, 1966, 351.

Vickery, B C: The future of libraries in the machine age. *Library Association record,* 68 (7), July 1966, 252-260.

Waite, C A: Books and the student: implications for the staffing of training colleges. *Education libraries bulletin,* 22, 1965, 1-23.

Webster, Felicia: *Library usage—a programmed textbook.* New York, privately printed, 1967.

Wendt, P R: New library materials and technology for instruction and research. *Library trends,* 16 (2), October 1967, 197-210.

Wendt, P R: Programmed instruction for library orientation. *Illinois libraries,* 45 (2), 1963, 72-77.

Wendt, P R and Rust, G: *Use your college library efficiently; a 530 frame program intended for high school and college freshmen.* Southern Illinois University, 1964.

Wilcox, Brian: The program: a means of increasing the efficiency of the text-book. *Library Association record,* 70 (12), December 1968, 317-320.

Wilson, L R and others: *The library in college instruction.* New York, H W Wilson, 1951.

Wojcik, M: Academic library instruction. *College and research libraries,* 26, 1965, 399.

Wood, D N: Instruction in the use of scientific and technical literature. *Library Association record,* 70 (1), January 1968, 13.

Wood, D N: Library education for scientists and engineers. *Bulletin of mechanical engineering education,* 8, 1969, 1-9.

Wood, D N and Barr, K P: Courses on the structure and use of scientific information. *Journal of documentation,* 22 (1), 1966, 22-36.

Wright, G H: Tutor-librarians in technical colleges. *Library Association record,* 63, September 1961, 314.

Ziman, J M: The light of knowledge: new lamps for old (the fourth annual Aslib lecture). *Aslib proceedings,* 22 (5), May 1970, 186-199.

Ziman, J M: *Public knowledge: an essay concerning the social dimension of science.* Cambridge University Press, 1968.

Index